Praise for THE POWE

The strength of this book is in its recovery of those principles of stillness and the contemplative life that are inherent in Restoration scripture and teachings. A practical guide to a dimension of discipleship too often lost amid the intense pace of church "activity."

—TERRYL GIVENS, coauthor of *The Christ Who Heals*

We have repeatedly been counseled regarding the negative consequences of living in a fast-paced, constantly plugged-in world, but the fact is that most of us don't know exactly how to extricate ourselves from all of it. We can't simply drop out of life. This volume is full of practical "hows" for living in this world while being more fully tuned in to the things of the soul. A useful and timely addition to the Latter-day Saint library.

—VIRGINIA PEARCE COWLEY, author of *Through His Eyes*

Consistently practicing the principles taught in *The Power of Stillness* has awakened my soul to the vastness and richness of living a Christ-centered life. I have found this kind of quiet "sacred stillness"—time communing with God—opens a reservoir of love, compassion, grace, and peace. These moments of intimate connection deepen and strengthen spiritual capacities that have helped me navigate every aspect of my life. The principles taught in this book, if consistently practiced, can be transformative.

—DEBI BARLEY, Latter-day Saint mindfulness teacher, Layton, Utah

The Power of Stillness demonstrates that mindfulness is implicit in the restored gospel and in life skills that are consistent with gospel living. Through numerous practical examples, it reveals how being still, present, and mindful opens us up more fully to the influence of the Spirit in various aspects of our lives. It reminds us of the message of so many ancient and modern prophets that when we are still we find God. I expect it to be a landmark in introducing mindfulness to more Latter-day Saints.

—JOHN T. KESLER, Director of Salt Lake Civil Network and Latter-day Saint Zen meditation teacher

For anyone who has felt inclined to engage in meditation and mindfulness but wondered if this is consistent with their own religious beliefs, *The Power of Stillness* provides profound reassurance. More than that, it makes a compelling case for ways that a mindfulness practice can significantly deepen spirituality within a mainstream religious life. Given the many benefits associated with mindfulness, reading this book could be nothing short of life-changing.

—VALERIE BENTLEY, PhD, mindfulness program expert

In these troubled times, *The Power of Stillness* reminds us how a quiet mind and open heart can help us find deeper peace, hope, and healing. I began a daily mindfulness practice when I was a young mother of a whole passel of small children. Alongside sacramental cleansing and temple renewing ordinances, this practice literally saved my life! I learned how to receive the gifts available to all who are willing to slow down and ask!

—SHAUNA MAY, wife, mother, stepmother, and grandmother

Living the principles taught in this wonderful book has brought balance and a quiet joy into my life in the gospel. We speak of "God's presence" as a place and state of being for which we must seek, and yet often forget that practicing our own quality of presence in our faith (by actually *being* present) will assist us with this. In the past I have wondered if there was room for me in our busy church to be a practitioner of mindfulness. Increasingly, I ask myself, "How can I live my faith fully *without* incorporating these things?"

—MARK DE ST. AUBIN, church member

Practicing the principles articulated in *The Power of Stillness* has deepened and enriched every aspect of my worship experience. Living increasingly in this way has helped me open my heart to receive the pure love and compassion that is at the core of the gospel of Jesus Christ, thus transforming my relationship with the Lord, with others, and with myself.

—RACHEL REIST, LCSW, mindfulness teacher

THE POWER *of* STILLNESS

THE POWER *of* STILLNESS

MINDFUL LIVING *for* LATTER-DAY SAINTS

JACOB Z. HESS, CARRIE L. SKARDA,
KYLE D. ANDERSON, TY R. MANSFIELD

Image Credits: page 3: Dan Piraro; page 16: John Kane/The New Yorker/Cartoon Bank; page 28: Ricardo Galvao; page 52: Mike Twohy/The New Yorker Collection/The Cartoon Bank/Cartoon Stock, www.CartoonStock.com; page 63: Mick Stevens/Cartoon Stock, www.CartoonStock.com; page 77: Patrick Hardin/Cartoon Collections, www.CartoonCollections.com; page 97: Kyle Webster/Cartoonist Correspondence; page 99: Mick Stevens/The New Yorker Collection/The Cartoon Bank; page 113: Leah Pearlman/Penguin Publishing Group; page 123: Lee Lorenz/The New Yorker/Cartoon Bank; page 140: Betsy Streeter/Cartoon Bank; page 158: Barbara Smaller/The New Yorker/Cartoon Bank; page 183: Bruce Kaplan/The New Yorker/Cartoon Stock, www.CartoonStock.com

© 2019 Jacob Z. Hess, Carrie L. Skarda, Kyle D. Anderson, Ty R. Mansfield

All rights reserved. No part of this book may be reproduced in any form or by any means without permission in writing from the publisher, Deseret Book Company, at permissions@deseretbook.com or PO Box 30178, Salt Lake City, Utah 84130. This work is not an official publication of The Church of Jesus Christ of Latter-day Saints. The views expressed herein are the responsibility of the authors and do not necessarily represent the position of the Church or of Deseret Book Company.

Deseret Book is a registered trademark of Deseret Book Company.

Visit us at deseretbook.com

Library of Congress Cataloging-in-Publication Data

(CIP data on file)
ISBN 978-1-62972-690-8

Printed in the United States of America
LSC Communications, Crawfordsville, IN

10 9 8 7 6 5 4 3 2

CONTENTS

ACKNOWLEDGMENTS

I extend deep gratitude to my wife, Monique, and mindfulness teachers Vicki Overfelt, Thomas McConkie, and (from afar) Jon Kabat-Zinn—along with Lou Bean, my high school creative writing teacher, for planting the earliest seed of my future passion for "conscious, affectionate awareness of the moment." Also, special thanks to Debi Todd and Davis Behavioral Health, for opportunities to teach and get trained as a mindfulness teacher, and to Rachel Reiss, Valerie Bentley, and the other Mindfulness-based Stress Reduction teachers in Utah for their support. And finally, appreciation to Michael Taylor for research assistance on the book and to Celia Barnes and Emily Watts for tough-love writing feedback and wise editing guidance.

—JZH

I am indebted to my wise mindfulness and meditation teachers, especially my Grandma Woolsey, who stayed fully present while playing endless rounds of catch with me, and my Grandma Ulrich, who made her home a peaceful and joyful "retreat center." I'm indebted to my parents, who inspired in me the desire and confidence to write, and to my husband and children for their unwavering support.

—CLS

I am constantly impressed and grateful for the courage and openness of so many to consider ideas that feel new and challenging. A special thanks to my wife, Jenny Wardle Anderson, three daughters, and extended family, who have been supportive of this project to invigorate lives and enrich faith.

—KDA

There are so many who have influenced and walked with me on this beautiful and unique journey—too many to mention—but I am first indebted to my wife and five children for their unquestioning support, patience, and presence. A special thanks as well to Jackie Halstead, whose presence inspired and taught me that there was a world of wisdom in the contemplative traditions, which ignited a journey to know God in deeper ways. Thanks to all the mindfulness and gospel teachers along the way whose lives have blessed and shaped mine.

—TRM

INTRODUCTION

NOT FEELING IT ANYMORE:

Little Time, Little Space, Little Spirituality

There's so much good in the gospel.
What's wrong with me that I feel so burned out?

One of the most dramatic portrayals of the redemptive power of stillness is hidden in an ancient story familiar to all Christians.

A woman, caught in adultery, is brought to Jesus by people ready to participate in one of the most extreme displays of power—taking someone else's life. Confronted by these indignant accusers, the Lord doesn't try to overpower them with dramatic words or shouting. Nor does He step away in fear—although the crowd could have become a danger to Him as well.

Instead, He holds still. And "as though he heard them not," Jesus "stooped down" to the ground, where He wrote with His finger in the dust. As the agitated voices around Him persisted in demanding an answer, the Savior remained fully calm. He then offered some few, quiet words—just a single sentence.

Then He bent down again to the ground. More than simply His words, something about the Lord's presence in that moment stilled and softened the crowd to the point that they dispersed entirely (John 8:3–10).

There are moments in our lives when we are also confronted with a cacophony of noise and demanding voices. For contemporary Saints, it's no longer a literal mob scene demanding our attention, although intensifying schedules and busyness can start to feel like one.

You likely know how that bombardment feels. You've also probably seen in your own life how stress creates havoc for sleep, emotions, physical health, and relationships. Does a frenetic way of living have spiritual consequences for us too?

Yes, it does. This book was originally inspired by how much we coauthors felt the cumulative effects of busyness and noise draining our emotional and spiritual health. Let's be honest: whatever goodness, beauty, and power can be found in a personal connection with God is *pretty hard to find* if we can't even bring ourselves to genuinely stop and be still.

But there is a stunning antidote! Instead of turning to caffeine and other stimulants to get through a dark or dragging time, many are finding that regular doses of something else can work wonders: a little more silence and stillness.

In addition to being happy Latter-day Saints, we have come together as authors from a shared background of professional training to help stressed-out people learn how to practice more of this stillness in their lives—something we've experienced in our own lives for many years as well.

Scared of Silence

As simple as this kind of an adjustment sounds, the truth is that some find more silence and stillness terrifying—even painful. One Harvard study found that two-thirds of men and one-fourth of women were willing to voluntarily shock themselves (ouch!) rather than sit in silence in an empty room for fifteen minutes with no distractions.[1]

Even those who *want* opportunities to stop, though, are finding it increasingly difficult, with 40 percent of the U.S. workforce spending

fifty hours at work per week, and almost 20 percent upwards of sixty.[2] In his best-selling book *In Praise of Slowness: Challenging the Cult of Speed*, Carl Honoré writes: "Speed has helped to remake our world in ways that are wonderful and liberating. Who wants to live without the internet or jet travel? The problem is that our love of speed, our obsession with doing more and more in less and less time, has gone too far, it has turned into an addiction, a kind of idolatry. Even when speed starts to backfire, we invoke the go-faster gospel."[3]

If you're being chased by a T-Rex, *"must go faster!"* makes a lot of sense. But does it really have to apply when shopping at the grocery store, or finishing a conversation, or "getting through" a bedtime story? Even "normal" activities are often being experienced too intensely, with one study finding that commuters commonly report greater levels of stress than fighter pilots and riot police.[4]

Rather than resting more to compensate for this increased pace and sheer amount of stressors, we're also sleeping and vacationing at historically low amounts—especially in the United States. For instance, the average American gets 2.5 fewer hours of sleep per night than a century ago[5]—with more than 87 percent of teens in one U.S. study getting insufficient sleep.[6]

When we *do* finally have a chance to rest and relax more, what do we do with that time? Harvard political scientist Robert Putnam found that since 1965, Americans have gained approximately six hours a week in added leisure time due to technological advances, with "almost all six of those additional hours" going to "watching TV."[7] (And that was before Facebook, Instagram, and Angry Birds.)

Elder Patrick Kearon summarized the bombardment: "Our smartphones, our computers, and our tablets are constantly buzzing, beeping, and vibrating with every new text, social media update, email, and photograph."[8]

More and more. Faster and faster. Less rest. More stress.

The effects on our physical and emotional health are increasingly clear. As depression researcher Stephen Ilardi notes, the human body was "never designed for the poorly nourished, sedentary, indoor, sleep-deprived, socially isolated, frenzied pace of twenty-first-century life."[9]

Exhausted and stressed people can also drag family relationships down as well—sometimes strained to a breaking point. Other effects are far less obvious.

On-Demand Spirituality?

In remarks to one of our wards recently, Bishop Jason Summers noted, "If we want to watch something, we can pull it up immediately on YouTube; if we have questions, we get immediate answers from Siri, or Google; if we want to talk with someone, there is instantaneous communication; if we want to buy something, we can order online and pick it up the same day." In so many ways, on-demand convenience is *so nice:* just like we want it and *when* we want it.

But what happens when things *aren't* like we want them? Are we still able (or willing) to sit with discomfort—to wait, to stop, and to be patient? Not always, right?

We believe this kind of a "microwave mentality" can introduce some unique difficulties for people of faith. Unlike polished marketing campaigns promising instant answers, God invites His children on a journey that involves exploration, curiosity—and struggle.

But when suffering, doubt, or conflict arise, they can increasingly feel intolerable: *I shouldn't have to put up with that, something is wrong . . .*

"Not Feeling It" at Church

Those stepping away from faith communities often report coming to feel that their experience has become rigid, narrow, overpaced, and so forth. Though the larger stated reasons for leaving often go beyond this, the joyless, day-to-day grind can become an ever-present reminder that fuels the ultimate decision to walk away.

Even so, many will admit that there used to be a richness to the life they are now leaving. Somehow, though, that sweetness is now gone. What more is there to say?

Maybe a lot!

Compared with a once-soulful experience of prayer and scripture study, many of us know what it's like to find these spiritual practices becoming impoverished, superficial, and thin. Although it's easy to conclude that prayer or scriptures themselves are somehow limited, it would be shortsighted not to also consider ways in which all of these larger tendencies toward distractedness, stressful busyness, and an accelerating pace of life might be playing a role.

Interestingly, the roots of the Chinese character for *busy* (忙 *máng*) point to some of the deeper effects of an over-hectic way of life: namely, *the death or loss of the heart.* Could we be "losing the heart" of our spiritual practices in large part through the exhaustion and frenetic pace of our modern lives? If so, what kinds of changes does this call for?

Stopping as a Radical Act

To start, we might ironically first need to *stop*. But, immersed in nonstop news and entertainment, many find it a lost art to be able to pause and deeply rest. Have you noticed how getting in even fifteen minutes of reading can seem almost impossible these days? Rather than blame a "boring book," maybe this says more about us.

If that's true, what would it mean to experiment with fresh, creative ways of approaching our lives?

Reaching a better place may not be as impossible as we may imagine. One thirty-something couple wrote about remembering a time "when things did not move quite so fast. When it wasn't expected that everyone was reachable at all times."

Finding a better balance doesn't mean "sitting in a rocking chair on a farm for twelve hours a day," they added, but rather finding a healthy pace of life filled with good accomplishments, without simultaneously feeling like "we're constantly drowning. Shouldn't that be a reasonable thing to want?"[10]

We think so.

Welcome to the New Counterculture

Given these broader trends, it's perhaps unsurprising that a new revolution is afoot in America and the Western world as a whole. Rather than opposing technology or efficiency or work or stress (all of which can be welcome parts of life), this is an uprising against the depletion of our inner world when any of these come to dominate our attention.

This revolution invites people to slow down, stop more, and cultivate more stillness and silence in their lives. "While the rest of the world roars on," Carl Honoré writes, "a large and growing minority is choosing not to do everything at full-throttle. In every human endeavor you can think of . . . these rebels are doing the unthinkable—they are making room for slowness."[11]

This hunger for more space is evident in popular books such as *Margin: Restoring Emotional, Physical, Financial, & Time Reserves to Overloaded Lives; Crazy Busy: A (Mercifully) Short Book About a (Really) Big Problem;* and *How to Have More Time: Practical Ways to Put an End to Constant Busyness and Design a Time-Rich Lifestyle.*[12]

While these books grapple with life in an accelerating society, other important questions remain: How is this hyperstimulated, rushed culture influencing how we experience the quiet message of Jesus? In what ways could it be changing our experience of gospel practices? And what happens when a certain spiritual practice doesn't "stimulate" us or "meet our needs" or "make us happy" in the ways we've come to expect with so many other things in our culture?

Exploring these questions may shed light on why some people are "not feeling it" when it comes to faith, while at the same time many others are feeling *more* enriched and restored as they approach these "same" faith practices.

Our experience has been that infusing any of these spiritual practices with more stillness, space, and silence changes them profoundly. Sabbath becomes more of a restorative retreat, temple worship a deep immersion into *non-doing,* and prayer a contemplative practice of quiet communion.

That depends, of course, on our being willing to approach these practices with fresh eyes—and perhaps even breaking from ingrained habits of efficiency.

Are you willing to become *even more* countercultural in this regard?

Mindfulness Defined

Central to this rebellion is something called "mindfulness" in the United States—reflecting an East-Meets-West love story in full bloom. Mindfulness has been defined as "paying attention, in the present moment, on purpose, and non-judgmentally."[13]

In its basic form, mindfulness is simply awareness—the skill of being aware of what's actually happening inside and around you: thoughts, feelings, physical sensations, and what the traditional five senses notice about the tangible world. This is an awareness of what's unfolding in the present moment, without overanalyzing the past or predicting the future. Thus, mindfulness has also been described as "conscious affectionate awareness of the moment."[14]

As you can see, this is not cold, robotic observing—it's noticing with compassion. Compared to the *death* or *loss* of the heart evoked by the Chinese character for *busy*, the character for *mindfulness* (念 *nian*) is a combination of two separate characters for *now* and *heart,* which, when combined, suggest *bringing the heart into the present,* or *the act of experiencing the present moment with your heart.*

Although many world religions emphasize the value of building this skill in the context of spiritual growth, mindfulness is most often associated with Buddhism because Siddhārtha Gautama was especially masterful in offering guidance for how to train and steady the mind. Jon Kabat-Zinn, an American physician trained in Zen meditation, helped translate these teachings for the Western world in 1979 when he developed a stress-management class to assist patients with chronic pain at the University of Massachusetts.

The Mindfulness Inherent in the Church of Jesus Christ

To propose, however, that members of The Church of Jesus Christ of Latter-day Saints need to look primarily outside of their own tradition for mindfulness would be to miss something big: namely, the degree to which invitations into mindfulness are *already* inherent within the restored gospel. Since Christ's teachings and relationships powerfully model stillness, pondering, reverence, full presence, and wakeful openness to revelatory insights, of course, it should be no surprise that these mindful skills and traits are also embedded in His restored Church.

But do we recognize them? Catholic leaders Thomas Keating and

Thomas Merton once described meditation "not as a newfangled innovation, let alone the grafting onto Christianity of an Eastern practice, but rather, as *something that had originally been at the very center of Christian practice and had become lost.*"[15]

It's been remarkable to see how much mindfulness is already threaded throughout Latter-day Saint faith and practice, even if we don't always realize it. Each of us coauthors has felt for some time separate nudges to gather insights about mindfulness in the Church of Jesus Christ. Jacob was introduced to mindfulness by his neuroscience adviser in graduate school and fell in love enough to train as a teacher and explore ways this could help deepen healing from depression. Carrie felt spiritually prompted to study mindfulness during a divorce. She has found it helpful in navigating a difficult calling, reducing back pain, and negotiating significant life transitions like having children and changing jobs—and she now shares it with clients as a therapist. Ty felt prompted to "learn meaningful solitude" during graduate school in Texas—and was subsequently introduced to mindfulness as a mental-health intervention. After finding the practice spiritually transformative, he trained as a teacher and shares it with his clients in therapeutic practice. Kyle first found mindful approaches early in his youth within the pages of traditional Chinese philosophical texts before later rediscovering it as a professor with his students in Kentucky, practicing meditation, yoga, and *qigong* as ways to nurture quietude and compassion in the face of life's many demands.

Although we've relished many of the authors exploring contemplative Christianity,[16] we also recognize that their language can be difficult for Saints to appreciate and understand. For this reason, we've aimed for this book to be a kind of translation for our own faith community. Each chapter takes up one deeper aspect of this exploration.

Ultimately, our hope is to advocate for and to help foster a meditative space where Latter-day Saint doctrine and language are embraced as a foundation of the practice—and where teachings from Joseph

Smith, David O. McKay, and Gordon B. Hinckley can help illuminate words from Jon Kabat-Zinn, Thich Nhat Hanh, and Thomas Keating (and vice versa). As John Kesler, one of the most seasoned and well-respected Latter-day Saint mindfulness teachers, has said, "I believe that The Church of Jesus Christ of Latter-day Saints has the potential to engender the most profound meditative tradition in the world."[17]

As a way to illustrate interesting synergies between different traditions, we will be quoting from Latter-day Saint leaders and authors as well as teachers within or inspired by the Buddhist mindfulness and Christian contemplative traditions. Our aim is not to systematically present a complete system of mindfulness, as much as to convey the spirit of the practice and highlight ways in which our existing faith practices could be experienced more richly with a little more space, stillness, and silence.

At the end of each chapter, we've included some "Things to Try," describing what the ideas discussed could look like in "real life." (For a growing list of more formal guidance and additional resources consistent with prophetic teaching, visit MindfulSaints.org.) As we will relate from our own life experiences, the gospel of Jesus Christ can look and feel remarkably different as it's infused with greater stillness, silence, and space. We're convinced that this can deepen and enrich the faith of many active Latter-day Saints. And for people who have at some point walked away from an impoverished experience of Latter-day Saint practices, mindfulness can also introduce new enriching and nourishing possibilities. We also hope that the larger mindfulness community not identifying as religious may benefit from understanding a uniquely Latter-day Saint perspective on mindfulness, with the many interesting synergies that exist between "the doctrine and the dharma."[18]

Ancient Things Brought to Light

One reason we can be open to new light as a people is that this is our religious heritage—a faith founded on an openness to *all* truth and inspiration. There is a strong sense from prophetic teaching that, in addition to dispensing truth, the Church is to be a receptacle of truth as well. For instance, the Prophet Joseph Smith taught that "one of the grand fundamental principles" of our faith "is to receive truth, let it come from whence it may"—encouraging the Saints to "gather all the good and true principles in the world and treasure them up"[19] as a part of the Restoration. Saints anticipate that some of the additional restored light will be a return of ancient wisdom, even a restitution of all things, "all the hidden mysteries of my kingdom from days of old" (D&C 76:7).

President Brigham Young similarly called it the business of Latter-day Saints "to gather up all the truths in the world . . . to the Gospel we preach, . . . to the sciences, and to philosophy, wherever it may be found in every nation, kindred, tongue, and people and bring it to Zion."[20]

Where the Power of Stillness Can Take Us

Let's return for a moment to the story with which we began: Jesus and the mob. As the scene wraps up, the angry crowd slows down, listens, reflects, . . . and walks away. Not because of tear gas or brutal force, but due to the power of the Lord's calm and compassionate presence.

And what remains after this amazing demonstration of true power? One man and one woman, sitting quietly in the dirt. In that moment, Jesus acknowledges the woman—really *sees* her. He sees her sin, He sees her potential, and He shares with her a profound moment of true connection as He frees her from the past. And she recognizes Him as her personal Savior.

This is where the power of stillness can bring us—into an intimate, personal relationship with the Savior Himself.

Let's begin.

CHAPTER 1

DOING:

Getting the Gospel Done

"Beware the barrenness of a busy life."
—SOCRATES

THE PROBLEM: *Jess pulls into the church parking lot, turns off her car, and sits back. As she thinks about the Young Women presidency meeting she's headed to, and all the things it will inevitably add to her to-do list, she slumps in her seat. "Come on, Jess—focus! You're early—how can you use this time?" Feeling spiritually sluggish lately, she'd set a goal to read a chapter a day from the Book of Mormon—starting with a prayer. "Okay, let's do this," she sighs, trying to motivate herself. Sitting taller, she mutters a quick prayer and pulls up the scriptures on her phone. "Oh, great, it's a long one." Just as she gets started, a text pops up on her screen. "Ugh, who is texting me right now?" It's her ministering sister inviting her to the temple Saturday. She slumps again. "That's my only time off—and I was really looking forward to having a break. But I do have to get that name done my aunt gave me." A feeling of tension and guilt floods through her. "Okay, yes, FINE, I'll do it!" she shouts out loud. The time is slipping away, and she hasn't finished the chapter. "C'mon, let's just get this done," she grumbles, scanning quickly. But time is up. Walking into her meeting, she starts to tear up. "These are all good things, so why am I feeling so burned out? What is wrong with me?"*

Overview

Sometimes we talk about gospel living as a set of *things to do* or *accomplish*—which can lead us to potentially experience the practice of our faith as unending activity or work. Unsurprisingly, such a consuming focus on doing more (and more) can create an impoverished experience of faith, characterized by superficial motions that drain the joy from worship.

We sometimes try to dig ourselves out of feeling spiritually drained by doing (even) more. If that doesn't work, we might feel stuck, concluding either that the Church "formula" isn't working so it must have been wrong to begin with or that "something is wrong with me."

When our lives are too full, we don't always have room to take in new insight, reassurance, or comfort from God. Counterintuitively, doing *less,* and consciously creating even-a-little-*more* space, may be key to sustaining vibrant faith in our accelerating society today.

The restored gospel already has mindful stillness built into its practices and teaching. Rather than relishing abundant opportunities to pause, catch our breath, and drink in Christ's "living water," however, we often end up approaching these sacred practices as just *more things to do.* Shifting how we talk and think about these gospel practices may help us personally rediscover their redemptive power.

Gospel Busyness

Elder Dieter F. Uchtdorf once recounted a fictional story of a Latter-day Saint couple explaining to someone what the Church asked of its members, mentioning "Church callings, home and visiting teaching, full-time missions, weekly family home evenings, temple work, welfare and humanitarian service, and assignments to teach. Also," they continued, "every six months our Church members spend a weekend attending or watching 10 hours of general conference."

The couple went on, "We haven't even mentioned family history, youth camps, devotionals, scripture study, leadership training, youth activities, early-morning seminary, maintaining Church buildings, and of course there is the Lord's law of health, the monthly fast to help the poor, and tithing."

The man said, "Now I'm confused. Why would anyone want to join such a church?"

President Uchtdorf then witnessed of the abiding joy that millions of Saints have found in yielding their hearts to God through these kinds of activities.[1] Even so, the fact that we *do so much* has led some to joke that *LDS* stands for "Latter-day Sprinters"—with others questioning whether Latter-day Saints are trying to "work their way to heaven."

For those who reach a point of exhaustion, however, this is no joke—prompting wonderings like: "Is this what God *really* wants for me? Will I be able to even keep this up?"

Doing Our Religion

The word most often used among Saints to describe a faithful member is *active*—compared with others who are *less active* or *inactive.* We also commonly summarize the gospel as a set of actions or behaviors—repentance, prayer, missionary work, callings, church and temple attendance, and so on.

In an accelerating world, however, what Elder David A. Bednar called "our lengthy gospel 'to do' list" can start to pose some unique challenges when we fail to note that something *deeper* is supposed to be happening *within* (and *through*) the doing. Elder Bednar says:

> In our customary Church vocabulary, we often speak of going to church, going to the temple, and going on a mission. Let me be so bold as to suggest that our rather routine emphasis on going misses the mark. The issue is not going to church; rather, the issue is worshipping and renewing covenants as we attend church. The issue is not going to or through the temple; rather, the issue is having in our hearts the spirit, the covenants, and the ordinances of the Lord's house.[2]

Mindfulness teacher Jon Kabat-Zinn has wondered whether we ought to relabel the species "human doers" rather than "human beings." This "doing mode of mind" can significantly influence our personal and community worship—potentially flattening and diminishing its power. But does it really *have* to be that way?

Not Doing Enough

Elder Richard G. Scott once shared: "Many voices from the world in which we live tell us we should live at a frantic pace. There is always more to do and more to accomplish. Yet deep inside each of us is a need to have a place of refuge where peace and serenity prevail, a place where we can reset, regroup, and reenergize to prepare for future pressures."[3]

Rather than prioritizing refuge, our tendency is often the reverse. Sister Sharon Eubank has acknowledged, "I am a maximizer, so I tend to think if one is good, five is better, and ten is best, and then I am completely overwhelmed." And Sister Reyna Aburto has also spoken of creating long lists for herself on the weekends that never seemed to relieve the pressure, saying, "I felt that I was never done."[4]

We have often heard the private cries of people for whom a sense of never being able to do or be enough has left them feeling hurt and alienated from God. And yet, in some cases, well-intentioned leaders have advised overwhelmed people that the solution is to "do" more. As

"I had an epiphany."

a local leader asked in one of our wards, "What is your temple attendance? Double it. How much time do you spend visiting? We've got to double it."

Sometimes more effort *is* needed, of course. But other times *more* doing might step beyond the "wisdom and order" of the gospel (Mosiah 4:27)—leaving people depleted and spiritually vulnerable.

Flattening Worship

A young Latter-day Saint mother recounted: "[I was] going *going going,* serving as Primary president, doing everything, involved in everything, volunteering for everything, and feeling. So. Tired. My thought processes were along the lines of 'I must not be praying enough. Or serving enough. Or reading my scriptures long enough.'"

After she had pushed herself to the point of contracting mononucleosis, her husband one day said, "This is *not* what Heavenly Father expects of you!"

Author Wendy Ulrich notes, "God doesn't burn out or use up one person to 'save' another, that's just not God's economy."[5] Pastor

Christopher Ash argues that when we serve or take on more than God has actually assigned us, without acknowledging our limits and need for rest, we are demonstrating a distrust in God's ability to "handle it" without our "help." He calls rest "an exercise in trust," adding, "God has already appointed his Messiah, and he did not appoint you."[6]

Although all believers *know* such divine help exists, our customary language often directs attention largely to our own actions. For example, instead of communing with God, we speak of "getting a chapter done," "saying a prayer," or "doing a session." In what ways might this kind of language inadvertently change what we're actually hoping to experience?

Too Busy to Receive Anything New

We often speak of Nephi's prophecy about future Christians saying they already have enough good in their lives, with *no more* space for anything else (see 2 Nephi 29). Yet when consumed with our own over-scheduled lives, don't we sometimes fall over this same *no-more-space* stumbling block, thus limiting whatever additional light God might have for us personally?

A story is told about a Zen master meeting his eager student for the first time. As they sit to talk, the master starts pouring tea until the cups are full. But he keeps pouring. As the student watches the tea pour all over the table and onto the floor, he finally asks, "Why do you keep pouring when the cup is already full?" The master responds, "That overfull cup is like your overfull mind. There is no room for me to add anything. You have to empty your mind if you want to take in anything I have to offer you."[7]

Do you know what it's like to have an "overfull mind"—to the point that there's simply no room for anything more? Citing the limited handcart space that forced earlier Latter-day Saints to leave some things behind, Elder Jeffrey R. Holland reflected that we may also need to ask what can truly fit in our own finite "handcart" space, and what needs to be tossed off. He suggested that "maybe a lot of other less-needed things [can] sort of fall out of the wagon."[8]

In one translation of Paul's letter to the Philippian Saints, he states that Jesus "emptied himself" so that He could do the work of the Father (Philippians 2:7, New English Translation). In our own communion with God, it may require a similar emptying of ourselves—our minds, our stories, our expectations of what "should" be happening—in order for us to be taught and tutored by Him. Admittedly, as seen in the story of Mary and Martha (see Luke 10:38–42), sometimes it can be *really good* things (how about serving dinner to the Lord Himself?) that lead us to be so "cumbered about much serving" that we're hardly able to sit at His feet and relish His words anymore.

The Restoration Mindfulness Advantage

And this is where the Church of Jesus Christ deserves a little (or a lot) more credit. In our attention to the many needful things *to do* as members of Christ's Church, sometimes the many excuses Saints have to *stop doing* are overlooked. Compared to a typical modern schedule, think of all the opportunities we have to stop: the Sabbath, personal prayer and scripture study, family meals, family prayer and scriptures, date night, family home evening, sacrament, the temple, and more.

Wow! *Every one* of these events is a prime "stopping time"—especially *if we approach it* in that way. Rather than a divinely prompted pause in our stream of doing-many-other-things, however, these sacred practices often still remain *just-one-more-thing-to-do.*

What would happen to us emotionally and spiritually if we approached these spiritual practices (each of them) as intentional moments of respite and sanctuary?

Instead of "all these things to do," imagine approaching each of these sacred practices "on purpose, in the present moment, non-judgmentally, as if our lives depend on them."[9] In this way, we can come to experience:

- What it feels like to kneel before God not simply to say more words—but also, to rest in His presence in stillness and silence.
- What it's like to sit down as a family not simply to "get a chapter done"—but instead, to hold scriptural text as an anchor to focus minds and hearts and facilitate an ongoing exploration about God's hand in our lives.
- What it's like to go to the temple not to "do a session"—but instead to *stop doing*—and to enjoy being in the haven of God's home, pondering His creative work in the world and in our lives.

None of these possibilities, of course, are foreign. References to a spacious, heart-full approach to gospel living are laced throughout scriptural and general conference teaching. But that doesn't make it easy to practice! As President Gordon B. Hinckley said:

> We live in a very mad world when all is said and done. The pressures are tremendous. We fly at high speeds. We drive at high speeds. We program ourselves. . . . But there is hardly time to reflect and think and pause and meditate. I daresay that most of those in this room today have not taken an hour in the last year to just sit down quietly, each [one individually] . . . reflecting upon his place in this world, upon his destiny, upon his capacity to do good, upon his mission to make some changes for good. We need to. I recall so vividly President McKay in his old age in a meeting with his counselors and the Twelve saying, "Brethren, we do not spend enough time meditating."

"I believe that with all my heart," President Hinckley added, while also acknowledging, "Your needs and your tastes along these lines will vary with your age. But all of us need some of it."[10]

Do *you* have some of it? The good news is that mindfulness is absolutely everywhere within the restored gospel, as long as we are willing to recognize it.

As Brother Michael Taylor, a research assistant for this book, reflected: "Mindfulness and contemplative prayer have made more difference in deepening my spirituality, life satisfaction, and marital happiness than anything else in the last few years." But then he added: "What surprised me was when I realized so much of it is already in Latter-day Saint scripture. *But I didn't see it.*"

Neither do many in the world recognize this, instead parodying the Saints as driven by doing. And that is a tragic irony.

Maybe this is just *one more reason* to move beyond our identity as *More*-mons!

Latter-day Saint Mindfulness Lingo

One reason that the mindfulness of Latter-day Saint living sometimes remains hidden is that we have a different language to describe how to cultivate stillness. For instance, the Latter-day Saint version of "practice mindfulness regularly" sounds more like "read the scriptures and pray daily." Our version of "it's really valuable to prioritize regular retreat" is instead, "be in the temple often." "Pondering" is also typically used instead of "meditation," and "reverence" instead of references to silence or stillness. Once we begin to translate into familiar terms, the powerful parallels become evident. Listen, for instance, to President David O. McKay's teaching here with that lens:

> The greatest manifestation of spirituality is reverence; indeed, reverence is spirituality. Reverence is profound respect mingled with love. . . . Reverence directs thought toward God. Without it there is no religion. [11]

Gospel Living as Ongoing Contemplative Practice

Rather than incessant excuses to "keep going" and "keep doing," then, so much of Latter-day Saint faith practice can be legitimately experienced as ever-ready excuses to *stop* meaningless busyness, and instead to *sit* with loved ones, *sit* with neighbors, and especially to *sit* at the feet of our Lord and His Father . . . whether or not dinner gets done on time!

Rather than something to "finish," prayer can thus become a sacred practice of personal retreat. Instead of something to "get through," scripture study can be a divine communion assisted by His words. And the Sabbath itself can become a relished mindfulness retreat happening each week, right within the walls of our own homes and chapels. In each case, these practices can become life-changing anchors in a larger culture swirling around us with hurricane force. As Elder Scott has also taught, "Without these regular practices it will be difficult to find the desired and much-needed peace and refuge from the world."[12]

In all these ways, rather than merely expanding activity or busyness, living the gospel can be experienced as a set of deeply restorative practices that help to cultivate more stillness in our lives—and all the divine inspiration and intimacy that can arise from *just a bit more* calm and space.

THE PRACTICE: *Jess pulls into the church parking lot, turns off her car, and sits back. As she thinks about the Young Women presidency meeting to which she's headed, and all the things it will inevitably add to her to-do list, she slumps in her seat. Closing her eyes and taking a deep breath, she pauses, noticing the tension in her stomach and shoulders. As she creates space for these sensations, the tightness eases some and she opens her eyes. "Hmmm . . . I'm early, how can I use this time?" She's been feeling spiritually sluggish lately, so has been paying more attention to small opportunities for connection with Heavenly Father. Sitting taller, she pulls up the Book of Mormon on her phone. Starting to read, she stops and remembers, "Wait." Closing her eyes again, she expresses thanks to Father for having a moment to spend with Him before her meeting. Pausing, she observes the quiet stillness in the car, verbalizing a desire for her heart and mind to be open to the Spirit as she reads a little. After another pause, she feels prompted to ask for help to be receptive to suggestions about how she can navigate this spiritual slump, before closing her formal prayer.*

She opens to the chapter she left off on and begins reading when a text pops up on her screen. "Ugh, who is texting me right now?" The irritation at the disruption flares through her. It's her ministering sister inviting her to go to the temple Saturday. She notices a heavy feeling accompanying the thought, "I was really looking forward to having a break Saturday morning; it's my only time off." She notes her resistance, "That's interesting that I'm having such a strong reaction to this." Her eyes fill with tears as she realizes how tightly packed her schedule has been lately, and how out of control even small changes can make her feel. She acknowledges what she's noticing compassionately, without trying to minimize how challenging things have been. As she sits in that awareness, the quiet thought comes to her mind of how she asked Heavenly Father just now to help her be receptive to His suggestions. She looks down at the text and feels touched as she reads the invitation to come to the temple. This time it feels like the text is directly from Heavenly Father. "I've been looking for opportunities to connect with Him. Spending Saturday morning in the temple sounds really nice." She texts yes, along with an enthusiastic, smiling emoji. Walking into her meeting, she tears up, laughing a bit that she didn't read any scriptures as she'd planned, but recognizing that this inspired "interruption" left her feeling very loved.

Things to Try

Build moments of stillness into the rhythm of your day—placing intentional interruptions into the normal flow of relentless activity. For example, after completing one activity, pause before beginning the next, using the transition time between activities as a chance to breathe a little. Notice what it's like to *not* jump immediately into the next thing (and to not fill the downtime with "busy" distractions like mindless grazing or checking your phone for no reason).

Experiment with consciously scheduling downtime in your calendar—slimming down your commitments and seeing what it's like to have more bumper room between activities. To avoid overbooking, carefully consider the (often overlooked) preparation time that requested commitments will need before saying yes.

Notice how often you are "pushing through" busyness. Signs may be a numb sense of being on autopilot, tension in the shoulders or eyes, a low-grade level of dissatisfaction, irritability, or relentless thoughts of being behind. Observe these feelings, thoughts, and sensations with compassion and curiosity.

Consider experiences like church and temple attendance, partaking of the sacrament, and prayer as opportunities to *stop doing*, rather than just increasing activity. Leading up to these activities, try some things to intentionally still your body and mind:

- Sink into your seat, letting the distractions flow around and through you—and feeling the contact of your body with the chair or floor.
- Notice your breathing more consciously for a minute, letting your attention rest on the physical sensations associated with the in breath and out breath.
- When you take a moment to pray or read scriptures, pay attention to how much of your internal focus is on *getting this done.* Experiment with relaxing a bit and easing into a deeper immersion, less concerned with time.

When feeling the weight of life on you, it can be helpful to focus for a short period on what's going on in the body:

- Bring attention to the physical sensations connected to your breathing for a few moments.

- Slowly scan the body for pleasant and unpleasant sensations.
- Note any areas of particular tension or pain—for example, "Hmm, there is tension in my stomach and shoulders."
- Especially when you are hurting or anxious, attend to the details of your experience with tenderness.

CHAPTER 2

NON-DOING:

Retreat and Sanctuary in the Restored Church

"Be still, and know that I am God."

—PSALM 46:10

THE PROBLEM: *"Let's go, GO, GOOOO!" The Sunday rush is in full swing at the Olsons'. Karen throws power bars at the kids while Richard frantically looks for the checkbook so he can cross "pay tithing" off his list. Arriving late, they rush into the chapel frenzied, shushing the kids, one of whom is . . . missing his shoe? They are forced to sit in the back by Brother Myers, who's already giving their kids "the look" for being noisy. Richard quickly shoves tablets to the kids. Feeling self-conscious and harried, he barely registers that the sacrament is being passed.*

Half listening to the talks, Richard and Karen get the gist of the messages—"do more." Checking her email during the closing song, Karen is caught off guard when it's time to head into her lesson, which leaves her feeling more anxious.

In the hall, Richard runs into someone to whom he's been asked to minister and learns that the family needs some help Tuesday. He is fast to volunteer but grumbles to himself, "How can I sneak in a ministering visit between work and Young Men?" Before he can figure that out, he sees a bishopric member out of the corner of his eye and hurries off, determined to turn in that tithing envelope.

After church, Karen and Richard collapse on the couch and wonder: When can we get away?

Overview

Sometimes, following God may actually involve doing *less*, rather than *more*—with value in making space for periods of retreat, as Jesus Himself did. The Sabbath and the temple offer unique, ongoing retreat experiences for the Saints.

There are unique ways in which worship services in the Church of Jesus Christ invite a cultivation of mindfulness. For instance:

- Distraction or boredom that may arise when listening to simple, unpolished messages can be part of valuable practice wherein we bring back the wandering mind again (and again) to recenter—similar to how meditation trains attention.
- The sacrament can be experienced as a uniquely restorative meditation introduced by the Savior Himself.
- We can also practice full, mindful presence at church through hymns, prayers, and our interactions with one another.

Throughout the rest of our week, we can then find ways to bring stillness into the rhythm of our lives, consecrating even a small piece of the "best time" of our day to the Lord. In this way, we can also cultivate sanctuary in our own homes—as best we can, creating an atmosphere of nourishing haven and retreat.

The temple can also be experienced as a profound retreat involving fully embodied, inspired meditation in connection with sacred ordinances.

Doing a lot of things sometimes feels so good and satisfying, right? Yet with busyness a badge of honor in society today, it's rare that any of us stop to question: hold on, who says God always wants *more*? Could our doing *more* at times actually *not* be what God wants?

Obeying God by Doing Less

Brigham Young once taught, "This is the counsel I have for the Latter-day Saints today. Stop, do not be in a hurry."[1]

Easier said than done, right? Maybe, like other things, this non-hurried-living will take some *practice.* But how? One of the classic practices in all contemplative traditions is getting away from the hustle-bustle "doing" of life and retreating enough to get into a deeply restful place of "non-doing."

President M. Russell Ballard offered encouragement to "be still and listen" as a way to better understand God's will: "We simply have too many distractions to capture our attention, unlike any time in the history of the world. Everyone needs time to meditate and contemplate."[2]

He added, "Even Christ, at the height of His mortal ministry, found time to stop and engage in purposeful periods of solitude."

During particularly difficult times, President David O. McKay would leave Salt Lake and retreat to his beloved hometown, where he could "be by himself" and "away from all the people." An assistant said of this retreat: "I'd take him to the Huntsville house . . . make a fire and he'd just sit in front of it when he was particularly weighed down with problems."[3]

On a few occasions, we have experienced more formal seven- and ten-day silent retreats. These are always challenging experiences as we lay aside the hurried, pressed madness of daily living to do the simplest of things: watching, listening, hearing, and seeing.

No talking. No phones. No writing. No looking others in the eye. Only intentional, continual quiet.

By the end of these retreats, we come away feeling clearer, more energized and hopeful—more like *ourselves* and in tune with the divine.

All because we stopped for a time.

It's rare, however, that anyone has the luxury of going on an extended retreat. How, then, can we build more of this quietness into our regular lives? As Saints, we already have three "retreats" built into our worship practice: the Sabbath, the home, and the temple.

Sabbath as Mindfulness Retreat

Despite a prophetic reemphasis on the importance of the Sabbath, it's common for many to end Sunday callings, visits, meetings, family gatherings, and wrestling with kids feeling more exhausted.

How could this day become more life-giving, cleansing, and retreat-like?

How about learning to deeply rest—pushing back on the relentless momentum of life in order to truly experience a rejuvenating pause? Scholar Adam Miller writes: "The Sabbath is God's way of interrupting our lives. It's his way of interrupting time, of breaking its spell. With the Sabbath, God introduces a hiccup into time, a beat of stillness, a little pocket of eternity."

Like God Himself, we can "bring the world to an end every seven days," as Miller puts it,[4] and use the Sabbath to celebrate the end of our own work.

Creating still spaces on the Sabbath to savor our relationships with God and our loved ones takes intention and practice. After one especially exhausting Sunday, one of our families decided to start protecting the day more—trying to make it more of a legitimate retreat:

> *Alongside various smaller adjustments like stepping away from email, news, and social media, we looked for ways to block off more time for just sitting together and talking or reading—even opting out of some of the family gatherings so we could have a little more space. The result was new refreshment flowing from the Sabbath—far more than we had experienced previously.*

Sometimes the way we begin the day can set the tone. In response to the common pattern of waking up too late, rushing with baths and getting kids dressed, and trying to get out the door to (hopefully!) make it to church on time, we've experimented with building more stillness into the morning routine as a way to set a different tone. After specifically waking up earlier for some early morning time to pray and meditate, we've found that having kid-free time to commune more intimately with God leaves us feeling more filled rather than rushed in the morning. We've also been intentional about waking up kids a little earlier to allow for a slower-paced morning, thus creating a Sabbath energy that ripples throughout the day.

Brother Mark de St. Aubin similarly writes about adopting a practice with his wife of "taking time on Sunday to be silent with one another—turning off even music and allowing our home to be a silent place for a few hours." He reflects:

> When we can do this, it feels like we are fasting from the usual chatter and junk food that the world and our own monkey mind provides in order to enjoy instead a quiet oasis from sound, communication, and chatter. It allows for my mental digestive system to come to a place of rest and feels like the kind of welcomed renewal for which the Sabbath was intentionally designed.[5]

What could discovering deeper Sabbath rest mean for your own life? If you move in this direction, don't be surprised if you get hit with worries about "being unproductive" or "wasting time" that could otherwise be put toward accomplishing something else. That's normal for anyone trying to make more space. Resist those voices! Something beautiful lies beyond them.

This is something different from pursuing "vacation time" or finding some way to entertain ourselves. As Christian author Henri Nouwen writes:

> We say to each other that we need some solitude in our lives. What we really are thinking of, however, is a time and place for ourselves in which we are not bothered by other people, can think our own thoughts, express our own complaints, and do our own thing, whatever it may be. . . . But that is not the solitude of John the Baptist [and other ancient disciples]. For them solitude is not a private therapeutic place. Rather, it is the place of conversion, the place where the old self dies and the new self is born, the place where the emergence of the new man and the new woman occurs.[6]

Wrestling the Kids

While the idea of the Sabbath as a retreat may sound inspiring, as anyone with children knows, there are sometimes special ninja moves required even just to get through church! Like many families, ours have often taken for granted that kids need "something to do" during church. Despite an abundance of crayons, books, and snacks, however, the kids in one of our families were so irritable and noisy in sacrament meeting one Sunday that we started wondering whether the very things designed to occupy them in church were having an opposite effect: reinforcing distraction and inattention.

So we tried an experiment:

> *What would happen if we didn't bring all the extra stimulation to church with us? All of a sudden, we saw our children sitting. Uncomfortably—obviously wanting the distractions back—but slowly learning to be okay without constant stimulation, getting better and better at resting in stillness.*

Sometimes, of course, the kids just won't settle, and that's part of the practice too. After one challenging Sunday, Carrie wrote:

> *Kids. Interrupt. Every. Two. Seconds. They don't care if you're sick, if you're busy, if you've got an important deadline, if you're really in the flow of what you are doing . . . they do not care. And they definitely don't care that the sacrament is supposed to be Mom's quiet meditation time with Jesus. But meditation is not about uninterrupted laser focus. It's a cyclical process of getting distracted, catching the distraction, and coming back to awareness—which helps me not lose my mind during the sacrament: "Mom, the Cheerios fell all over the floor." (Okay, full disclosure, Fruit Loops.) "Mom, make me a paper airplane." "Mom, I want to sit next to you, Kevin won't let me sit next to you, scoot OVER, KEVIN!" "Mom, Dad is asleep." "Mom, why did Jesus die anyway?"*

Of course, this kind of distractibility is not limited to just the kids!

Sunday Worship as Sitting Practice

We've all experienced it: sitting in church, listening to the speaker and having our mind wander.

Don't we sometimes assume that our obligation is simply to soldier on, trying to do our duty—even though it's hard and, well, "I'm not getting much out of this." We may also get irritated about our boredom or critical of the speaker . . .

Other times, of course, we simply catch our drifting mind and bring our attention back to the speaker, doing our best to listen some more—until the attention wanders again.

Interestingly enough, this is one of the *core skills* taught in formal mindfulness training. Rather than somehow getting the mind to *stop,* it's about noticing when your attention has wandered and then gently, compassionately escorting the mind back to an anchor point—usually the breath or body (in this case, the speaker). Then repeat.

Physical sensations in the breath or body as a whole aren't necessarily "exciting" either—but they *don't need to be* in order to anchor mindfulness practice. And Latter-day Saint worship, with its simple, unadorned operations, provides another great opportunity for intensive, regular mindfulness practice (more so, in fact, than if it were dramatically entertaining). Christian leader Parisa Parsa notes, "Church services are one of the last places left to gather for non-commercial reasons not centered on entertainment."[7]

Again and again, we can bring our attention back to the talk, the words of a prayer, and the music. The placement of hymns right before prayer creates a unique opportunity to steady and calm our minds for what comes next.

Rather than being only spectators, of course, everyone has the chance to share, be heard, and grow among the Saints. That means we *all* get practice listening to common people who are often unpolished, and we learn to hold a loving, forgiving space for each other as brothers and sisters.

In a recent combined priesthood meeting, one of us walked in to find thirty-five men in rapt attention to the speaker:

Not a single cell phone was out. These men who could have been watching football at home were all listening carefully to another plain-spoken brother counseling them on how to become better husbands and fathers. I had a clear sense that I was witnessing something remarkable.

We've also noticed a difference in our conversations at church when we approach the interaction as an opportunity to practice meditation, with the "anchor" being the person with whom we're speaking. When we bring a full, calm presence to the small interactions with our brothers and sisters, whether shaking hands and catching up or coordinating administrative logistics, we find ourselves better connecting with people, even though the words exchanged are no different from before.

These are things we practice *every week* as members of the Church: quiet presence and compassionate attention.

Our Most Precious Mindful Practice

Similar to Christians the world over, we join in a very simple practice that Jesus Himself taught all His followers: bringing our hearts and minds together to focus attention for a short period of time on an ordinary piece of bread and a small drink of water.

In this moment we renew not only our individual covenants with God but our collective sense of unity with one another as His covenant people. More than just a nice little ritual, this mindful practice is described by the Lord as "a commandment" that He pleads with us to "always do" (3 Nephi 18:12).

President David O. McKay taught, "The short period of administering the sacrament is one of the best opportunities we have for . . . meditation"—in particular, a chance to "meditate upon his goodness."[8]

More than a hope to experience His presence in the week ahead, it's clear that in that very moment, God intends for something to happen. The scriptural record notes that "they were filled with the Spirit" after partaking of the bread and wine—a filling that is clearly more than simply physical (3 Nephi 20:9).

Elder Dennis B. Neuenschwander thus taught: "Sacrament meetings are really more than just meetings. They are sacred moments in a holy place."[9]

Fighting for a Little More Space the Rest of Our Week

In all these ways, the Sabbath can become a regular retreat to rest our hearts and minds deeply. What about the rest of our week? As prophets have encouraged for many years, our experience has been that even little steps toward more silence and stillness—retreating *just a bit* from the hustle on a daily basis—can be life-changing.

It was Jesus who encouraged people to intentionally get away from the rush of life to be with God: "Enter into thy closet, and when thou hast shut thy door, pray to thy Father . . . in secret" (Matthew 6:6). Sometimes finding space takes fighting for it a little—pushing back on the colonization of our minds and hearts by foreign distractions or aggressive demands, kind of like boxing out for a rebound in basketball.

C. S. Lewis taught: "The real problem of the Christian life comes where people do not usually look for it. It comes the very moment you wake up each morning. All your wishes and hopes for the day rush at you like wild animals. And the first job each morning consists simply in shoving them all back; in listening to that other voice, taking that other point of view, letting that other larger, stronger, quieter life come flowing in." He adds, "We can only do it for moments at first. But from those moments the new sort of life will be spreading through our system: because now we are letting Him work at the right part of us."[10]

Do you know what that feels like—to wake in the morning to a sense of demands and deadlines so tangible that you feel them in your gut? Next time that happens, see what it's like to push back a little and find some space to breathe.

For some, the best time to reground is first thing in the morning, while others find this deeper stillness in pauses during the day or in the lull before bedtime. The exact time may be unique to our body's rhythms and life circumstances, but when we consecrate a piece of our "best time of day" to the Lord, He can touch that time, like He did the few loaves and fishes, and create a soul-nourishing bounty beyond what we would expect in mere minutes.

Home as Our Primary Sanctuary

Although sweet retreat can happen at an office or anywhere, there are two places we relish most as centers of Latter-day Saint stillness, sanctuary, and retreat. After speaking of the universal need "deep inside each of us . . . to have a place of refuge where peace and serenity prevail" within our frantic larger society, Elder Richard G. Scott went on to teach that "the ideal place" to find that refuge and peace was "within the walls of our own homes."[11]

President Russell M. Nelson has likewise called our homes "the primary sanctuaries of our faith, where each can be safe from the sins of the world."[12] If for many of us our homes may feel a long way from that sanctuary, moving in that direction can be a practice in itself—consistent with President Nelson's encouragement to "diligently work to remodel your home into a center of gospel learning."[13] Consistently, one of the priesthood ordinances Latter-day Saint families are invited to participate in is the formal dedication of their homes "as sacred edifices where the Holy Spirit can reside and where family members can worship, find safety from the world, grow spiritually, and prepare for eternal family relationships."[14]

Quiet places in and around our homes can become sacred to us as well. President Gordon B. Hinckley was fond of sharing the story of his elderly father, who lived in a home with a rock wall on the grounds: "It was a low wall, and when the weather was warm, he would go and sit on his wall. It seemed to me he sat there for hours, thinking, meditating, pondering things."[15]

Temples as Sanctuaries for Revitalizing Retreat

The temple is another place of sanctuary where we can retreat, stop, and be still. Yet our language about temple experiences can sometimes inadvertently send a different kind of message. For example, we normally talk of "temple work" and "doing a session" or "doing baptisms" or "doing a name."

Clearly, sacred ordinances are the central, precious focus of temple practice. But the varying attitudes we bring with us into the temple can influence, even change, what we experience there. When we approach the temple as something to "get done," rather than as a chance to *lay aside* all the busy doing of our lives, we can miss out on experiencing our time there as a joyful respite.

Perhaps, then, we could approach the temple as, among other things, a veritable Latter-day Saint Meditation Center.

Certainly, part of that peace arises from the relative silence, stillness, and solitude of the temple—qualities shared with all mindfulness centers. Distinctive to temples, however, is the offer of a unique kind of relational meditation in a house claimed by God Himself. In ancient scripture, the temple was described by Jehovah as a house where "mine eyes and mine heart shall be there perpetually" (I Kings 9:3).

As we leave the worldly confusion behind and enter this sacred space to reconnect with the Lord, we can experience a mental and emotional settling. President Boyd K. Packer described, "At the temple the dust of distraction seems to settle out, the fog and the haze seem to lift, and we can 'see' things that we were not able to see before and find a way through our troubles that we had not previously known."[16]

Even that work we often joke about *just to get to the temple*—pushing back on different responsibilities, arranging things at home—could be embraced as anticipatory clambering that makes the sweetness of the temple hush even more vivid. And then inside, rather than simply getting through a session, we can sit with temple teaching like ancient poetry. Instead of just rehearsing words mentally, we can let ourselves rest in a place deeper than thought and participate in ordinances as full-bodied experiences.

The positive impact of these experiences is not just some mystical abstraction. Many research studies have demonstrated that a focused period of meditation thickens parts of the brain responsible for concentration, decision making, and awareness, while shrinking other parts responsible for fear responses.[17] The results are a sense of groundedness and an ability to respond to stress from a deeper, wiser mind-set. Along with the still focusing of the mind, the temple adds to these benefits by activating the symbolic, creative, and intuitive right brain.

In all these ways, the temple can, quite literally, help heal our weary souls and stressed brains—both spiritually and physically. After retreating to the temple, we can then return to our daily lives and problems with fresh energy and creative insight previously untapped.

No wonder President Spencer W. Kimball loved the poetic invitation engraved on old English churches for all entering a temple: "Enter this door as if the floors were paved with Gold; And every wall of jewels all of wealth untold; As if a choir in robes of fire were singing here; No shout nor rush, but hush, for God is here."[18]

THE PRACTICE: *"Let's go, GO, GOOOO!" The Sunday rush is in full swing at the Olsons'. Karen throws power bars at the kids while Richard frantically looks for the checkbook. Gathering at the back door, they pause. Karen and Richard look at each other and smile, squeezing hands briefly before folding arms. As is their norm, they take a breath and allow things to settle for a moment before offering a quick prayer. Feeling a little more stilled, Karen opens her eyes and notices something. "Michael, where's your shoe?" Richard hunts down the missing loafer while Karen buckles the kids into their car seats.*

As they approach the building, the kids run ahead. "Whoa, guys, wait up!" Karen stops the kids, and they pause before going inside. "We're going into sacrament meeting now—let's get our bodies calm, okay?" She prompts them to "blow some imaginary bubbles" (that is, take some deep breaths) before going inside. Looking around, they find a seat beside Brother Myers, who's already giving them "the look." Richard smiles kindly and detects a compassion for the man in the midst of his self-consciousness. As he listens to the sacrament prayers, he allows himself to hold this mix of feelings, and brings his attention to the moment . . . the words, the silences interrupted by little noises, the physicality of eating and drinking the bread and water. . . . When their littlest gets rowdier, Karen pulls him onto her lap and softly whispers to him to help him refocus.

As the speaker begins, Richard feels a heaviness he recognizes as boredom, and he has an urge to check his email. But instead of reacting, he notices these sensations, then turns his attention more deeply to the speaker and the moment as it unfolds. During the closing song, Karen feels a sense of unity and love as she joins voices with her brothers and sisters.

On the way to Sunday School, Richard chats with the Nelsons. When he sees a bishopric member out of the corner of his eye and remembers the tithing check in his pocket, he notes a flare of distraction, but returns his attention to the older couple. Their sprinkling system is on the fritz, and they're wondering if he could help on Tuesday. He quickly agrees, but as they continue to chat, he feels a tension in his shoulders and realizes he is clenching his jaw. Curious, he turns to his thoughts, "How will I fit in a visit between work and the youth activity?" At a pause in the conversation, he asks them if he could come by on Saturday morning instead, and they agree that will work. After exchanging a funny story, he continues to class, smiling.

Karen and Richard come home and sit together on the couch feeling full and satisfied. Just then Richard notices the envelope in his pocket—the tithing check! The flash of irritation dissolves as he sees Karen laugh and shake her head with humorous acceptance.

Things to Try

Sit down and look at your actual calendar, mindfully observing what fills your time. Consider what motivates various activities—could some goals be better achieved by *doing less*?

Experiment with approaching the Sabbath day as a refreshing "retreat" from patterns in the rest of the week, providing a long block of time to pare back activity, noise, doing, digital distraction, and so on. If slowing down for the whole day seems too daunting or unrealistic at first, set aside a few hours, or even just one hour, for designated "non-doing" time.

Rather than multitasking during the speaking and singing of a meeting, try more of a full-body immersion in worship, leveraging different elements of the service as mindful touchstones allowing you to better anchor your attention within the present moment. When the mind wanders off, recognize this not as a problem but as an opportunity for valuable practice: noticing where your attention has gone, and then gently guiding it back.

Rather than giving children things to keep them busy or occupied during church services, experiment with tapering back on the distractions in a way that lets your children learn to be okay with *not* being entertained and occupied.

Explore ways to deepen your experience with the sacrament as your preeminent mindfulness practice of the week. In addition to reflecting on covenantal promises, let the details of the ordinance itself ground your attention when it wanders. For instance, you might:

- Visually follow the sacrament tray as it makes its way to your hands.
- Hold the cup and bread in your fingertips a little longer than you are used to, feeling their weight and noticing the texture of the objects between your fingertips.
- Notice the sensations as the bread and water pass between your lips and into your body.

- Listen to the clinking of cups and trays punctuating the silence of the ceremony.

In casual conversations at church, listen with full attention. Make eye contact and really see the person with whom you are speaking. Grant the moment your undivided attention, even when the topic discussed is ordinary and time is short.

When you find yourself feeling frazzled and thinking "I need a break," approach the temple as a profound immersion in non-doing—allowing you to step away from relentless activity and busyness into something else entirely.

CHAPTER 3

COMMUNING:

Like One Person Talking to Another

"Prayer is not monologue, but dialogue; God's voice is its most essential part. Listening to God's voice is the secret of the assurance that He will listen to mine."

—ANDREW MURRAY

THE PROBLEM: *Justin brushes his teeth while watching the clock. It's getting later, and the fatigue of the day is wearing on him. As praying crosses his mind, he thinks, "What's the point? If it's just going to be another empty, twenty-second telemarketer exchange with God, there's no sense in burning what little attention and time I have."*

Prayer used to feel more effective, deep, and meaningful for Justin. However, relentless worries and responsibilities had crowded that old lane to God over the years, making prayer now just another guilt-tinged item poking out of the crush of tasks to accomplish.

Even so, crawling into bed, Justin mutters a prayer in his mind: "Heavenly Father, thank you for this day. Thank you for my many blessings. Please help me have a good night's sleep and a good day tomorrow . . . " Before he gets to "Amen" he slumps over and drifts off to sleep.

Overview

Even those who have spent a lifetime seeking God experience times when prayer feels mundane, shallow, and empty. Reexamining how we approach and think about prayer can open us to new insights and create space for us to get "unstuck" from hollow prayer habits.

Christ prepared for and sustained His very difficult ministry by regularly retreating in solitary communion with Heavenly Father. His practical example demonstrates how we can build our own spiritual resiliency, thus staying engaged in the difficult work Heavenly Father may require of us.

Rather than something to repeatedly accomplish or get done, prayer can be experienced as a sacred, mindful practice—bringing the body and mind to a pause, noticing what's going on inside, directing (and redirecting) attention to God, and seeking to soften and yield our hearts.

Creating more silence for quiet reflection within our conversations gives Heavenly Father space where He can do His work and helps us receive direction we encounter in that divine silence (while compassionately noting partial answers and continued limitations in our understanding). Like a fire that warms the body, this kind of prayer warms the soul.

Meaningful prayer doesn't always have to be eloquent, lengthy, or deeply philosophical. Prayer can feel as familiar and nourishing as pausing, with full presence, to receive a hug from a beloved, wise friend. Simple "daily bread" prayers also have a valuable place at the table.

No matter how long someone has sought to follow Christ, there are times (for all of us) when prayer can feel mundane, shallow, and empty. When God does not seem to be listening, when no answers are coming, we can defeatedly wonder, "What's the point?"

"It just stopped being meaningful to me. I couldn't feel anything anymore," a woman attending one of our workshops relayed in a discussion on prayer.

In such moments, some may conclude that prayer no longer "works"—and leave it behind like an outdated device. But rather than looking for an upgrade, could we find a way instead to deepen, refresh, and reimagine what this experience of prayer is?

Through our own experiences getting stuck in unsatisfying prayer, we've found that stepping back and noticing our assumptions and approaches to prayer with fresh eyes can open us to new insights and enrich our prayer practice.

Prayer as a Personal Retreat

There are no "one size fits all" solutions to carving out time for deeper experiences with meditation, pondering, and prayer. But we've noticed that when we look at our schedules with fresh curiosity, unnecessary time drains become more visible and small, creative windows of opportunity emerge.

A little more quiet can go a long way. As the poet Rumi wrote, "The quieter we become, the more we can hear." With excitement in his voice, President Henry B. Eyring once said the following about hearing the voice of God: "Every time it happens, I was quiet inside. . . . *so* quiet . . . then I could hear it. I realize if I had been noisy in terms of my thinking, then I couldn't have."[1]

It's not the quiet alone that is powerful. Rather, the quiet prepares a space where God can work, along with a willingness to pause our own will and yield to whatever we encounter. We've seen how guided meditation can help clear out the clutter in our minds in a way that helps connect us with God more tangibly and meaningfully.

President David O. McKay taught that people would find "most inspirational moments" coming when "you are alone with yourself and your God." After characterizing meditation as a "form of prayer," he then described this as "one of the most secret, most sacred doors through which we pass into the presence of the Lord."[2]

That kind of meditative prayer may require a bit more silence and stillness than we're accustomed to. Sometimes we associate "talking less" with something uncomfortable—aka "awkward silence"—in conversations with others.

But it was none other than Jesus Himself who warned against our tendency in prayer to think we will be heard by God for "much speaking," "many words," or "being so wordy" (according to different translations of Matthew 6:7).[3]

This additional silence helps ensure that we aren't just hurriedly throwing up the first thing that comes to mind in prayer. As it states in the Bible, "Be not rash [or "impulsive" or "hasty"] with thy mouth, and let not thine heart be hasty to utter anything before God" ["nor be in a hurry to talk in God's presence"] (Ecclesiastes 5:2).[4]

So, what do we do in the space this new silence might bring? Cynthia Bourgeault writes of God "as a loving presence that was always near, and prayer as a simple trust in that presence." She goes on to describe the possibility of more stillness in prayer involving "a wordless, trusting opening of self to the divine presence," suggesting that this "is about the simplest form of prayer there is."[5]

If it's true that our love is reflected in that which we are willing to create space for (our kids, college football, reading scriptures), then prayer is a way to exercise and embody love, with God creating a space for us as we create space for Him.

Prayer and Jesus's Solitude

It's common for people contemplating the unique aspects of Jesus's life to presume they arose largely because, "well, He was the Son of God!"

While true, does that adequately explain everything? We often speak of all that Jesus *did* in His life—service, healing, teaching. But how about the different times when the Lord very clearly stepped away from the activity around Him to find a calm from which to commune?

The two examples of this we discuss most are the most dramatic and harrowing: retreats to Gethsemane and what President David O. McKay called "the mount of meditation where, during the forty days of fasting, he communed with himself and his Father."[6]

But Luke wrote that this kind of retreat to secluded places is something Jesus "often" did (Luke 5:16).[7] Sometimes it was to a mountain or a desert, other times to a garden or out on a lake. And as in our lives, these periodic retreats happened at different times in his day. Once He arose "a great while before day" and went off to a "solitary place" to pray (Mark 1:35), and on at least two occasions He found precious quiet time late into the night: "When he had sent the multitudes away, he went up into a mountain apart to pray: and when the evening was come, he was there alone" (Matthew 14:23; see also Luke 6:12–13).

Sometimes quiet time was prioritized *before* important occasions, such as prior to the Sermon on the Mount (see Luke 6:12). And on other occasions it followed major events. Right after the five thousand were fed, "Jesus went to the mountain for solitude." After Jesus heard about the murder of His friend and cousin, John, He also immediately withdrew Himself from the disciples and traveled "privately" unto a place variously translated as "solitary," "secluded," or "deserted" (Mark 6:32).[8]

And on one occasion when there was so much "coming and going" that His disciples didn't even have time to eat, Jesus invited them to join Him in getting away, saying, "Come ye yourselves apart into a desert [quiet, solitary] place, and rest a while" (Mark 6:31).[9] On that occasion, it's worth pointing out, other people foiled His retreat (as happens so often with us!), after they found out where He was going.

As Christian author Bill Gaultiere summarizes, "The priority of Jesus' solitude and silence is everywhere in the Gospels. It's how he began his ministry. It's how he made important decisions. It's how he dealt with troubling emotions like grief. It's how he dealt with the constant demands of his ministry and cared for his soul. It's how he taught his disciples. It's how he prepared for important ministry events. It's how he prepared for his death on the cross."[10] From His early retreat into the wilderness to His final, agonizing retreat in Gethsemane, some of the most important parts of Jesus's ministry involved stepping away to find *space to commune.*

We don't often say as Church members, "When life throws you a blow, take some private time for yourself. Go to a quiet place that you enjoy and step out of the demands of your life for a little while and regroup—*because that's what the Savior would do.*"

But He did. Rather than heal one more person, share one more meal, or teach one more sermon, how remarkable to see the Son of God Himself making precious time for retreat. This silence and stillness, of course, was not a neutral, empty space, but rather, one filled with an infusion of tenderness, communication, and connection with His precious Father. As Gaultiere says, "His time with Abba was one of the most important things to Him."

What does that mean for us? As Nephi might put it, if the Lamb of God, He being holy, should have need for retreat and communion, O then, how much more need have we? (see 2 Nephi 31:5).

Tender Intimacy with God

Elder D. Todd Christofferson wrote about being impressed by a comment from Bishop Desmond Tutu, the Anglican archbishop in South Africa, after he was asked this question: "Have you found that your relationship to God has changed as you've grown older?"

Bishop Tutu responded, "Yes. I am learning to shut up more in the presence of God." He recalled that when he was younger, he prayed with what he called "a kind of shopping list." But now, he said, "I think [I am] trying to grow in just being there. Like when you sit in front of a fire in winter, you are just there in front of the fire, and you don't have to be smart or anything. The fire warms you."

Referring to Desmond Tutu's comment, Elder Christofferson noted, "I think that is a lovely metaphor—just sit with the Lord and let Him warm you like a fire in winter. . . . Let that moment be one of rest and refreshing and reassurance and renewal"—with a hope that people might have "some sense of the beloved status you occupy as [the Lord's] son or daughter. I hope you will take time . . . to sit for a few quiet moments and let the Savior's Spirit warm you and reassure you of the worthiness of your service, of your offering, of your life."[11]

After Christ had completed His Atonement and Resurrection, He returned to the shores of Galilee and prepared a meal for His fisherman friends. It's tender to imagine the glorified resurrected Savior humbly gathering sticks, building a fire, and cooking fish to literally feed the disciples, serving them as He had His entire mortal life. Sitting with Him on the ground in these very ordinary surroundings, yet surely in reverent awe, these disciples were fed, warmed, and loved. And then they were encouragingly taught and called to service themselves. The mood is calm, full of forgiveness and attentiveness.

Our prayers can be this intimate. This nourishing. This meaningful.

And they can happen in the middle of real life. One young mother shared with us her experience of being home alone one day with a house full of small children, standing in the kitchen while her kids were "going crazy," running around, noisily fighting. The sink was full of dishes, the kids were hungry, and she was exhausted. Feeling overwhelmed and alone, she knelt down on the ground, right there in the middle of that kitchen mess, and prayed. Not a grocery list prayer of requests, just a "will you sit with me for a second because I'm losing it here" prayer. That moment of stillness, of reconnection with a loving presence, didn't include a lot of words, but it was a tender acknowledgment of both the chaos and Him. After this brief "prayer hug," she took a deep breath and resumed making lunch, feeling a little more stilled and centered. She quite literally fed her hungry sheep after having been fed by Him.

Prayer as a Practice

Rather than something to *get done,* prayer can begin to take on a life of its own. And, like real life, our prayer life can feel really messy sometimes. For instance, Adam Miller describes a moment in prayer when we get "caught up in thinking about something else and the brain browns out." Encouragingly, he writes that "the substance of a prayer is this willingness to remember, to heave your wandering mind back, once more, in the direction of God, and then, when it drifts off yet again, to heave it still another time."[12] One Christian leader from the Middle Ages, Francis de Sales, similarly taught: "If the heart wanders or is distracted, bring it back to the point quite gently and replace it tenderly in its Master's presence. And even if you did nothing during the whole of your hour but bring your heart back and place it again in our Lord's presence, though it went away every time you brought it back, your hour will be very well employed."[13]

That repeated bringing back and redirection of our attention is very similar to what happens in meditation, underscoring how prayer can be similarly approached as a rich practice—which is different from our common attitudes toward prayer. As Christian author John Eldredge once joked, "Honestly, people approach prayer like sneezing—you just sort of do it, and that ought to be enough. But prayer is something you learn, and grow into, and get better at, just as you do anything else in life that really matters."[14]

In the same spirit, after cautioning that prayer is so much more than "polite recitations of past and upcoming activities, punctuated with some requests for blessings," President Russell M. Nelson asked, "Are you willing to pray *to know how to pray*?" affirming, "The Lord will teach you . . . if we will humbly present ourselves before the Lord and ask Him to teach us."[15]

Some of the nuanced skills we practice in prayer include: formulating intentions, deciphering personal revelation, unifying ourselves with God as a co-creator, learning to experience our body as a temple of the spirit, resiliency in the face of doubt or confusion, personal introspection, humility, sanctification, patience, and how to bring God's healing and enduring power into our lives and the lives of those we influence.

When we recognize prayer as tutoring in this richly broad skill set, not just a means of getting "an answer," discomfort coming up or a surprising silence from God makes more sense. They're all part of a much bigger practice.

More Intention in Simple Prayers

Let's be honest: Latter-day Saints pray a lot!

We have personal prayers morning and night, we pray over every meal, we have couple and family prayers, we pray at the start of the two-hour church block, at the start of every single administrative meeting in church, and at the end of all of those meetings . . . and even within the meeting that opened and closed with prayer, we have more (sacrament) prayers. On a typical Sunday we could easily have engaged in a dozen prayers or more!

As much as we value prayer, the frequency and commonality of our prayer habits can sometimes unintentionally undermine the sanctity of this humble encounter with the divine. But does it have to?

On a recent trip to Jerusalem, Carrie had lunch on a sailboat on the Sea of Galilee. She recounts:

> *I sat with my girlfriends under a bright blue sky, dangling my feet into the sea, while one of Israel's top chefs brought course after course of absolutely amazing local dishes prepared right on the shore: fresh-caught fish, organic vegetables grilled on the open fire, beautiful salads, and rich dark chocolates. At the height of the deliciousness, some smiling, scraggly fisherman rowed by, saw our feast, and joyfully shouted a toast, "L'Chaim!" To Life!*

Now, that, *my friends, was a meal blockbuster.*

On another day soon after, for lunch I had canned tuna at my desk. Meh. That was a meal rerun.

Our body needs the nourishment of lunch, even if most of those meals are simple reruns. In some ways, the ordinary presents a neutral canvas so those extraordinary meals can really shine.

This is similarly true with prayer. Many of our prayers may feel more like canned tuna than sailboat dining, but our souls need the nourishment of those simple, everyday prayers, and in some ways, their ordinariness creates a baseline, allowing the more noteworthy prayers to stand out.

Christian author Tish Warren elaborates: "There are indeed moments of spiritual ecstasy in the Christian life and in gathered worship. Powerful spiritual experiences, when they come, are a gift. But that cannot be the point of Christian spirituality, any more than the unforgettable [meal] I ate years ago is the point of eating. . . . Thousands of forgotten meals have brought me to today. They've sustained my life. They were my daily bread."[16]

Despite all the ways religious practices are now disparaged in modern society, there's a power in regular, even ritualistic observance—yielding to a set way of going through something that creates a rhythm and muscle memory. As Elder Jeffrey R. Holland has pointed out, the word *religion* comes from the Latin word *religare*, meaning "to tie" or, more literally, "to re-tie."[17] We might then think of each prayer offered potentially tying and binding us closer to God.

Even "daily bread" prayers can have small moments of stillness. One family takes three breaths to help wiggly kids calm their bodies before family prayer. In a Primary calling, another has children practice "the skill of still," focusing on calming the body and listening to a moment of quiet before beginning a prayer in class. Rather than launch immediately into an opening prayer, we've also begun classes having people briefly check in with one another so that the person offering the invocation can include personal details about class members in the prayer.

President Spencer W. Kimball wisely taught that prayers should be "appropriate to the need. Certainly, it should not be long when little children are involved, or they may lose interest and tire of prayer and come to dislike it."[18]

Prayer as Monologue

When was the last time you knelt down, breathed deep, and then begged God to *make something stop* or go away or change? This kind of a plea for God to DO something is not uncommon: "Help my wife to . . ." "Guide us to know what more we can do to . . . " "Soften his heart." "Take this away!"

In these moments, we think of ourselves as being fully present with God. After all, we're focused, we're petitioning His attention, and we're very sincere in our request. So why does God feel so far away in such a needful time?

Perhaps God seems distant because we've fallen into using prayer to get *what we want*—and as a tool to make *our own agenda* happen. This kind of subtle aggression involved in trying to push God to "do something" for us also demonstrates an underlying anxiety and limited trust in Him. In this mind state, author Richard Rohr cautions, "you will not access the Holy because the only thing that gets in is what you already think, what you already agree with, and what does not threaten you." In that state, how can we possibly expect to receive more? And, as he puts it, "if you aren't ready for more . . . how can you possibly be ready for God?"[19]

Instead of opening ourselves to His will in this moment, we sometimes end up treating God like a genie in a bottle, or like Santa Claus: if we can just convince Him that we've been very, *very* good, maybe He will deliver that blessing we want so much. Noticing this same tendency in one of our families, five-year-old William asked after a prayer

"Anyway, we'd love to have You on board for the Creighton deal."

one day, "Why do we keep telling Jesus *what to do?* Are we Jesus's king? I thought He was our king?"

Rather than treating God (through prayer) as a means to our end—like a kind of tool for our purposes—we've found that our prayers substantially change when we start focusing on being a tool for *His ends.*

Prayer as Dialogue

Joseph Smith taught that part of the first principle of the gospel was "to know that we may converse with [God] as one man converses with another."[20] Elder Jeffrey R. Holland explained:

> So often we make prayer a kind of a laundry list of requests. It's sort of like we want to go to the store to get this and this and this—and I need it right now and I want it in the bag and I'm on my way. And we fail to remember that

> He's supposed to speak back to us. We'll finish a prayer and be up and on our way and back into the hubbub of the world. We need to let him speak to us, in a quiet setting, in a still setting. And that probably means after we're through talking (and I hope it's not just requests).

Listen to this next part: "When we're through talking, *we need His voice!* We need to provide an environment *for Him to speak to us.* And that means . . . *stay quiet. Stay silent.* Stay in a private setting. We often deny Him a chance to reply!"[21]

In an interview with Mother Teresa of Calcutta, Dan Rather asked, "What do you say to God when you pray?" Her answer seemed to surprise him: "I listen." "Well, then what does God say?" he added. With a smile, she said, "He listens."[22]

Thoughtful, mindful, reverent prayer is about cultivating a relationship with God as a real Being to whom we can speak genuinely, intimately, and personally. That two-way communication is a big part of transforming "saying a prayer" into "being with God."

President McKay's habit was to go into "a darkened room, a private room, . . . kneel in the center of the room, not on a chair, not against a bed—and he would kneel and *say nothing.* This is not at the end of the prayer. This is before the prayer started. He would say nothing for a matter of minutes until he felt like he was worthy to approach the throne of the Lord, to come before deity. . . . And then he would wait [after speaking] . . . and give the Lord a way to answer and speak back."[23]

Sometimes this means sitting heartfully present with Heavenly Father, in a state of patient not-knowing, for many years before specific answers emerge. But this holding still is not wasted time. Along with cultivating "general and loving awareness of the presence of God," this prayer, as Thomas Keating writes, is about "consent[ing] to God's presence and action within us" and "gently establish[ing] an attitude of waiting upon the Lord with loving attentiveness." Working at this very real practice of prayer reaffirms "our intention to place ourselves at God's disposal."[24]

In this way, we develop what Keating calls "the habit of surrender to God's increasing presence and action." As Christian author John Backman writes, "By sitting in silence, focusing our attention on the present moment and the Spirit within it, we provide space for God to speak gently to, and move within, our souls."[25] This cultivation involves staying aware of the play of our own desires and hopes in prayer, with an intention of yielding to higher desires and hopes whenever a discrepancy comes into view. As Keating adds, "sometimes our own gentle activity predominates, and at other times the Spirit takes over"—with the presence, influence, and power of the Holy Spirit growing over time in prayer.[26]

This shift in our prayers can be relieving and exciting. Rather than constantly trying to get God on board with Our Big Plans, we start to ground ourselves in the conviction that Father sees more than we do. If that's true, then our time with God becomes a constant inquiry to better understand and align ourselves with a will whose boundaries are forever extending beyond our own finite perspective—like the horizon on a mountain hike.

When compared with a *make it go away prayer,* this kind of "mighty" prayer involves a full presence that feels different: we are authentic and real with Him, even about our pain—but we are also quiet, humble, and reverent in His presence.

Rather than the same old ritual, this kind of earnestness opens up a rich variety of prayer experiences. For instance, voicing the confusion or pain that brings us to our knees may have a heart-aching intensity. Or, in less stressful periods, we may notice our hearts just feeling tired or heavy with everyday concerns. In happier times, our hearts may be bursting with gratitude. But in all cases, as we sit in His presence, fully there, surrendering our limited understanding and will to His, a more subtle experience with God unfolds. As we make space in our hearts for

His will, love, and wisdom, we begin to feel our way past our subjective biases, and we invite true intimacy with God. We begin to trust Him.

Rather than a duty or something to "get done," prayer can thus become a communing act of intimacy. Instead of an instrumental "tool" toward our favorite ends and agendas, this kind of prayer becomes a unification or at-one-ment—a way to consistently bring our heart and mind into alignment with God's, over and over . . . prayer by prayer.

THE PRACTICE: *It's Justin's thirty-minute lunch break, and he's dedicating half of it to sitting quietly in prayer. He decided to start this Monday and Wednesday habit when he realized mornings were too rushed to be still, and in the evening, he was too tired to concentrate. After finding the quiet bench at the edge of the duck pond on his work campus, he closes his eyes and makes note of what is happening in his mind and body. He takes some deep breaths and allows his focus to leave the work morning and the after-work plans and settle into this moment. He thanks Father for the chance to be here with Him, pausing as he allows the sensation of loving attentiveness in God's presence to grow. He hears the birds in the trees and feels the warmth of the sun on his back as he lingers in this feeling. When his mind wanders, he catches the distraction and gently redirects his attention back to the present. After fifteen minutes he ends his prayer, opens his eyes, and takes a deep breath, feeling refreshed, and starts walking back to work.*

Things to Try

Rather than something to get done or merely "say," experience prayer as a deeper, embodied practice by retreating away from noise and activity to commune with God. Consider approaching some prayers as one would sitting by a warm fire with a beloved friend—not with a wordy agenda, but with full presence and appreciation.

Especially when there's a lot going on inside, take some time before formal prayer to watch what's going on internally and better understand your current state before starting to express anything in words. You might also try some things to help the mind and body settle:

- Allow your body to settle deeply in your kneeling or sitting position, feeling the contact of the ground for a few moments. Bring your focus *beneath* the emotional or mental "noise" to a calm, centered space within.
- Sit quietly for a short time, noticing physical sensations throughout the body and whatever emotions are present as well.
- When thoughts or sounds distract, gently guide your attention back to the rise and fall of your own breathing.

When you do speak, let the words arise tenderly from your direct experience—observing and articulating, in the Lord's presence, what you're noticing in your mind, body, and heart. Pause between sentences or ideas expressed, maintaining heartfelt, inquisitive presence with anything that arises, as you listen quietly.

When the mind wanders in prayer, pay attention to where it has gone—considering whether it's perhaps not distraction but the influence of the Spirit that has guided it. If you find yourself daydreaming or ruminating, acknowledge the wandering, before tenderly guiding your attention back to God. Recognize this recalibration as an important, meaningful part of healthy prayer practice.

Notice where your heart is during prayer—the emotions behind the words. In particular, watch the tendency to treat God in prayer as a means to an end or a tool for your hopes and plans. When sensing that, consciously reaffirm your intention to be a tool for *His ends*. Allow prayer to become a more conscious, ongoing process of cultivating your heart and uniting yourself to God's desires.

When painful, intense, or heavy emotion arises, bring compassionate attention to it in prayer.

- Let yourself be curious about observing whatever is here, including discomfort—continuing to observe what's going on in the body and mind during the prayer.
- Be compassionate with yourself as you allow feelings to ebb and flow, exploring what internal resistance means with the Lord.
- Notice any impatience or sense of demand for a particular answer or timeline.

When there is no time in a given day, don't be defeated. Once in a while, reach out to Him as you would make a quick phone call to your best friend—the one who understands when you have to end the conversation abruptly because your child just spilled the juice or your boss just emailed. Let Heavenly Father know about the small joys or setbacks of the day—right as they're happening.

CHAPTER 4

QUIETING:

Working with the Restless Mind

"With some effort, we can stop the outer noise . . .
but stopping the inner noise is another matter."
—CYNTHIA BOURGEALT

THE PROBLEM: *It's Sunday afternoon. Miraculously, the baby went down for her nap without protest, and Jason and Lorna have an extra hour. Jason decides to spend some of this manna-from-heaven time meditating and praying, while Lorna turns her attention to the prophet's challenge to read the Book of Mormon. Jason turns on the fireplace and kneels in his living room, intending to sit quietly. But almost immediately his mind races in a hundred directions, even back into old sins and conflicts that stir up anger. "Grrr . . . what's up with that! This is not at all relaxing. Forget it." Lorna has a similar outcome sitting at the kitchen table. Only a few verses in and her mind wanders; she just can't concentrate. "What's the point? I'd be more productive doing the dishes." Two minutes later, with music and podcasts blaring, Lorna is at the sink and Jason is checking email.*

Overview

When we begin to build more intentional stillness into our days, it's quite common for inner noise to *increase* (at first). How we choose to *respond* to turbulent mental content makes a big difference in how quickly our calm and quiet will deepen.

By turning *toward* uncomfortable mental states, we can learn to work with them in different ways: creatively, tenderly, patiently. As we formally practice holding significant discomfort in a mindful place of deep calm and stillness, we develop the capacity to do the same when discomfort arises in our regular lives.

Noting the distraction and returning, over and over, to a chosen anchor can help quiet the mind. Such anchors might include our breathing, our direct relationship with Heavenly Father, the sensations of the Holy Ghost, and scriptures or prophetic text.

A lot of spirituality and Zion-building is simply hard. But the unexpected, mundane, and sometimes downright brutal mortal experiences we go through can involve just as much of God's presence and support as the pleasant, "warm fuzzy" ones do. Both Gethsemane and the Sacred Grove highlight the need and value of learning to hold both light and dark, the bitter and the sweet.

It would be nice if making more time for silence and stillness automatically brought restfulness and peace. For most, however, outer silence doesn't necessarily correspond to an inner silence. Christian author Cynthia Bourgealt writes, "Even when the outer world has been wrestled into silence, we still go right on talking, worrying, arguing with ourselves, daydreaming, fantasizing."[1] Seeking to cultivate more stillness and silence—including in our spiritual lives—often provokes resistance, with a remarkable level of push back arising internally.

But why? Shouldn't embracing deeper quiet be pretty straightforward and easy?

Stillness can be far more difficult than it first appears. In this chapter we'll consider well-established ways of working with resistance and inner turbulence so it doesn't end up controlling our decisions.

Noisy Inside

Many who step off the treadmills of their lives to cultivate more stillness do, in fact, initially experience a sense of slowing down and calm. But then, almost universally, people start to notice surprising levels of distracting emotions and "chatter" in the mind. One Latter-day Saint woman, juggling work and home, described a period of life when she felt "incessant noise and thoughts rambling through my head, no matter what." Whether she was in her "sacred space" of reading scriptures, at the temple, or playing with children, the mental content in her mind "played on repeat, *nonstop.*"

Little wonder people sometimes hesitate to be quiet—even avoiding something like prayer altogether. This is especially true for the many who have lived through painful traumas, and for whom ugly memories and flashbacks can sometimes arise spontaneously. In those cases, silence can feel almost re-traumatizing, as difficult thoughts or emotions can actually intensify. One young woman healing from past abuse told us that she avoids being still because that's when the terrifying thoughts get harder to deal with.

Sometimes the thought of taking time to be quiet can ironically increase our stress, as "one more thing to do." Elder Patrick Kearon acknowledges, "Just the mere suggestion that you might carve out some time from your already overscheduled day increases the sense of pressure you feel."[2]

In each of these cases, silence, stillness, and stopping are no simple matter. So, what is there to do?

Turning Toward the Noise

What if these un-relaxing experiences are, in fact, an integral part of cultivating more stillness? Indeed, staying present *in the midst* of whatever feelings and thoughts arise *is the point* of meditation. The intent is not to purge oneself from these or any other sensations in order to reach a state of calm, but rather to observe the full-spectrum inner activity of the mind and body from a place of acceptance and stillness.

Interestingly, a new level of stillness often reveals whatever is *already there*—including underlying turbulence and agitation that may have been unnoticed all along. But it's still up to us whether we want to face whatever emerges in the stillness—because, the honest truth is that we don't have to! We always have the option of avoiding, distracting, and pushing away from whatever's happening inside. Mindfulness, however, invites the opposite: turning inward *toward* the inner noise or turbulence.

As counterintuitive as it might sound, *turning toward* whatever is here (even if it is scary, or bothersome, or uncomfortable) is the beginning of deeper calm and stability—and it's what we would propose as the first, most basic step toward finding more internal quiet and calm. When we meet what is here, face it, and even confront it, something changes. Over time, suffering can decrease dramatically.

This doesn't happen at instantaneous, microwave speed, though, no matter what that nifty app you downloaded promises you. Patterns in the body and mind have a momentum that can be intense—which partly explains why they typically cannot be redirected through sheer willpower or one dramatic insight. Yet, as detailed in research about mindfulness, consistent practice over time can begin to change the "stuckness" of the body's reactivity, to the point that deep calm can begin to infuse all of our life experiences.

The path toward less chaos and noise inside, then, is one that can take practice and time to travel. As with most important things, a little preparation in advance can help catalyze things too.

Preparing the Unsteady Mind

In Jesus's visit to the Nephites, right after sharing beautiful, majestic teachings, He perceives that their capacity to receive them has waned: "I perceive that ye are weak, that ye cannot understand all my words." He then encourages them to go "unto your homes, and ponder upon the things which I have said, and ask of the Father, in my name, that ye may understand, and *prepare your minds* for the morrow, and I come unto you again" (3 Nephi 17:2–3; emphasis added).

When was the last time you prepared your own mind to receive, connect, or commune more deeply?

Our experience has been that seeking revelation can certainly be enhanced by employing methods to quiet and prepare the body and mind—like tuning an instrument.

For instance, there are many ways that we can enhance the quality of prayer along its edges, working with the space around the words we utter. We have found that a short period of intentional silence helps sharpen our focus for what follows, allowing us to take into our prayer an attunement of the ear and willingness to listen.

Sometimes logistical adjustments can also make a difference in predisposing our minds toward a better experience. Speaking of prayer, Elder Jeffrey R. Holland encouraged, "Really think through how you're going to do this—and what are some of the optimum benefits and circumstances that can provide that," recounting the following experience with his wife earlier in their marriage:

> We were finding ourselves having our evening, closing prayer . . . exhausted . . . and we could hardly stay awake. And we just decided, there's no requirement that this has to be a prayer at 11:00 at night when you can hardly form the words. And we just moved it up. We just took a time and said, "We're going to pray together earlier, and it won't be flopped against the bed or almost asleep by the time you get into the conversation with the Lord. . . ." And it really, materially changed our lives and our ability to make that evening prayer a meaningful experience with the Lord.[3]

"An interesting selection, Dad, yet essentially a failure—as you can see, I'm still awake."

As the physical body comes to a rest, there's still no guarantee the mind can do the same. Especially if we've lived busily in our heads all day, sometimes the activity can continue unabated as we lie down.

For that reason, another kind of more direct work is required.

Working with the Wandering Mind

Speaking of her own difficulties at bedtime, one woman said, "When I'm trying to fall asleep and my mind is going a dozen directions, simply coming back again and again to attention to my breath helps me relax and be still."

In an article titled "Finding Inner Peace and a Deeper Connection to Christ Through Meditation," BYU–Idaho professor Sheldon Lawrence acknowledges that "during prayer, it's natural for our minds to wander; when reading the scriptures, our attention often drifts to what we're going to do next. Not surprisingly, it's easy to feel spiritually empty and apathetic."

Sheldon went on to speak of the breakthrough of beginning to incorporate more intentional meditation in his life—not just pondering, but "a more intentional approach to bringing stillness and focus to our distracted minds" and a "purposeful cultivation of inner peace and quietude."[4]

Desperate to find some internal relief, the sister with the noisy mind downloaded a meditation app in hopes it could make a difference. Even while giving it an honest try, however, she confessed to getting frustrated at the beginning, feeling like she "couldn't keep 'focused' enough on the meditation to do any good." She added, "When my mind wandered, I would become upset and irritated. I just couldn't do it!"

Rather than assuming she was "failing" at the meditation, she eventually realized this is pretty much how meditation works—a cycle of focus, distraction, and refocus. Instead of trying to create a state of forced and rigid stillness, and feeling like she was failing when she couldn't sustain that, she started to *work with the cycle of the mind*—training it to recognize its wandering and consciously come back to a place of calm, back to still . . . over and over.

Learning to notice the drift of the wandering mind and guide it back to a single point is part of learning to "quiet" the mind. These moments of intentional stillness, practiced more regularly, helped this woman experience a deeper level of quiet, and what she called a "blessed peace" began to grow in her life.

As reflected here, a central part of working with the mind is having an anchor to help ground it—a "still, quiet place" to which your attention can return and rest at any point.

Anchoring the Mind

While anything can be an anchor for the mind to return to—the words of a song, the child you're playing with, a piece of bread or sip of water, or a certain phrase—the most common anchor is the breath itself. It was coming back to the breath that helped the woman with her mind "going in a dozen directions" eventually "relax and be still."

In President Russell M. Nelson's Christmas reminder about the broader extent of Jesus's message of repentance, he invited us to consider potential change in our deeper, internal experience of mind, knowledge, spirit—"even our breathing."[5]

In addition to being fantastically portable, the breath, for believers, references the life we are gifted by a God who is "lending [us] breath" (Mosiah 2:21). Although subtle, the physical sensations associated with the breath (or body) can be an elegant gateway through which we can bring ourselves to stillness and ground ourselves in the present moment.

Mindfulness is not about mere presence or stillness, however, but also about *what comes out of that stillness and presence.* And what is that? An awareness *deeper* than thoughts, emotion, and physical sensation—in which we can learn to rest and "watch" everything else happening around us. That awareness is what most meditators aim to find—what Dr. Amy Saltzman calls our "still quiet place inside."[6]

And what would Christians call this wise inner space? Our spirit! As we all know from our own experience, intimacy with our own spiritual core is very easy to lose. Learning to rest more deeply in our immortal, core spirit is the work of meditation, or what President David O. McKay called "communing with yourself."[7]

For Christians, finding a resting place in our own spirit is not sufficient, of course. The refuge we seek is not just connecting with our own breath, but abiding in the divine. As Brigham Young said, "I want to see men and women breathe the Holy Ghost in every breath of their lives."[8]

These different anchors for the mind need not be in competition. For instance, after grounding and stabilizing their attention in the breath, Christian meditators often redirect that attention to God in prayer.

While God and His Spirit are wonderful anchors to seek directly, they can sometimes feel elusive. That's one reason the words of the scriptures can be another helpful anchor for the mind—providing a little reality check outside of ourselves, with some accountability to whatever perceptions we currently have. As Christian author John Backman put it once, "Scripture is a wonderful tether. . . . One can go off on flights of fancy if silence is our only practice."[9]

Not Feeling Like Praying

Jon Kabat-Zinn encourages students to meditate, whether or not they feel like it—counsel not unlike Brigham Young's teachings about personal worship: "If, when the time for prayer comes, you have not the spirit of prayer upon you, and your knees are unwilling to bow, say to them, 'Knees, get down there;' make them bend, and remain there until you obtain the Spirit of the Lord."[10]

Many of us can relate to this situation President Young teaches about. Carrie describes a long period in her life when she couldn't bring herself to prayer:

> *In earlier years, prayer was a natural beginning and ending to my day, without a lot of conscious effort on my part. But in college, I got angry with God for not helping me in the ways that I so generously and neatly outlined for Him, so I decided that if He wasn't going to listen to me, then I wasn't going to talk to Him.*
>
> *After a period of not praying, my anger eventually faded to the point that God and I were on speaking terms again. However, the habit of daily prayer did not naturally resume. I tried to pray—I really did! I cajoled myself, bribed myself, chastised myself, guilted myself, set New Year's resolution pacts with close friends that I would do it, I even made sticker charts (oh yes I did!) to try to restart the habit. I believed in prayer. I valued it. I wanted to want to pray. But the reality was, I felt enormous resistance. I could not do it.*

She was not able to "goal set" or "push" her way through the resistance, so she *had* to approach this block to prayer in a new way.

She got curious.

Bringing Gentle Attention to Discomfort

One of the most beautiful aspects of mindfulness is its willingness to embrace the full range of human experiences, even deep, unrelenting resistance to prayer. That's just what Carrie did:

> *I softened my gaze, took some deep breaths, and leaned into my resistance with a mindful willingness to see whatever was really there. With this more tender, less judgmental mind-set, I was reading in the Bible Dictionary one day about prayer. (I could read about prayer, I just couldn't do it!) And these words stood out:*
>
> *As soon as we learn the true relationship in which we stand toward God (namely, God is our Father, and we are His children), then at once prayer becomes natural and instinctive on our part. Many of the so-called difficulties about prayer arise from forgetting this relationship.*
>
> *Since prayer was definitely not feeling natural and instinctive, I decided to meditate on my relationship with God. Mostly I saw God as, meh, sort of aware of me. But during that difficult period of my life, it felt like He had thrown me into the deep end of the pool so that I could "learn." The reassurance that "there are great lessons to be gained here" did NOT comfort me. I felt like I was drowning, gasping at God: "I can't trust You. I don't want to trust You! You don't really get me. Maybe You care in some big, cosmic way, but I'm drowning here and You're not doing anything to help! Never mind! Just stay away from me!"*
>
> *It made me cry to realize this was my belief about God. It was not my real belief. I should say, it was not what I was taught about God. But oh boy, you bet it was my perception. No wonder I was having trouble praying.*

Goal setting and bulldozers had not created the environment where this insight could unfold. Mindful curiosity and quiet, pondering meditation did.

This insight created space for me to approach God from a more authentic place. Now I could bring my fear that He was untrustworthy, and my hurt, into conversation with Him. I approached Him as I really was and created space to experience Him for who He really was, not just my guarded, distorted perception of Him.

What I experienced was His patient, enduring love. That *increased my capacity to tolerate the betrayals and confusing "lessons" of my mortality.*

It's really hard, dare we say impossible, to have life experiences go through us and not have them affect how we see God. Staying authentically, fully present in our relationship with Him, allowing ourselves to experience the full range of our reactions to Him, with mindful curiosity and wisdom, allows us to peel back and shed the disillusionment and false perceptions we cling to about God.

It took years for Carrie: *Let me say that again, it took* years. *But now I crave prayer and see it as a personally transformative means of experiencing divine love. And I don't even need sticker charts!*

Waiting for a Settling

This kind of insight won't arise if we walk away from discomfort in our quiet times. When students come across physical or emotional discomfort during meditation, Jon Kabat-Zinn invites them to "cradle the discomfort," reflecting the kind of tenderness and compassion that one can bring to difficult moments.

There is something to be said about committing enough time to see the wrestle through, as one bishop told us about spending longer blocks of time in prayer during a difficult period. He said: "That's the great thing about designating that time for prayer with a sense of conviction. Because then instead of inching toward it, you already clear out enough time to wrestle with yourself during the hour before God."

This naturally involves greater patience to wait upon the Lord, anticipating that things can resolve (more easily) if we give them a bit more space. Thus, Richard Rohr writes: "Do not try to settle the dust. Do not rush to resolve the inner conflict. Do not seek a glib, quick answer, but leave all things for a while in the silent space."[11]

Sometimes the internal voices are so loud and relentless, once again, that even a moment of inner calm is hard to come by. A lingering problem, a lurking obligation, unaddressed anger or hurt, guilt, building excitement, the residue of some medication, or even the lag of a powerful dream can make a search for calm self-reflection and restoration like sitting on a tossing train car. At these times, we sometimes believe our only option is to "stick it out" and endure bravely.

When confronted with this type of opposition, we have an alternative to stiffening our neck or running from the trouble. Sometimes we can simply observe the inner turmoil and abide it, rather than hardening to it.

Holding It All

We often narrowly define "spiritual experiences" as predictable and pretty encounters with the light. But a lot of spiritual growth is not soft and fuzzy, it's hard. Wrestling with God in the darkness; getting lost in the mists while being taunted; being an invisible outsider, only able to reach the hem of the One who could heal; the boring grind of walking across the plains toward a land you've never seen; being a parent responsible for a child whose mission you don't fully understand; weeping alone, while the friends who were supposed to be riding this out with you are literally asleep—these are spiritual experiences.

When a spiritual wrestle is intense, perhaps the greatest challenge is simply staying present. In fact, it's only when we embrace the whole experience that the ordinary is truly transformed into the sacred. Joseph

Smith's first verbal prayer started out as a typical spring day with an unremarkable teenager kneeling not far from his own backyard. But by enduring the subsequent crippling darkness, as well as the incredible intimacy of seeing and being seen by God, Joseph experienced a transformation of the ordinary. If Joseph had not stayed present with these intense and unexpected realities, not to mention the plainer routine aspects of his life's mission, the fulness of the Restoration could not have unfolded.

Once Joseph took his question to Heavenly Father, of course, the light did not immediately flick on. He hit resistance: overwhelming, real, knock-you-to-the-ground darkness. Compared with any other moment (in which attention to God may feel somewhat easy), Joseph's account illustrates the degree to which staying present to God in a moment of despair can require substantial effort—even "exerting all [our] powers" (Joseph Smith—History 1:16).

Christ's atoning event, which we look to and celebrate as triumphant, also centered on our Lord's willingness to *be present* to the darkest of dark and the most bitter pain ever endured. Only then, in experiencing them, did our Savior receive the eternity-changing power to succor us through our own awfulness.

Both Gethsemane and the Sacred Grove highlight the crucial capacity to endure both light and dark, to experience the discomfort that often lurks around the edges of anything potentially sweet. This at times includes tolerating the painful questions, the unconventional (and sometimes only partial) answers, periods of threatening darkness, and the intensity of being tutored by God.

THE PRACTICE: *It's Sunday afternoon. Miraculously, the baby went down for her nap without protest, and Jason and Lorna have an extra hour. Jason decides to spend some of this time meditating and praying, while Lorna settles at the kitchen table to read the Book of Mormon.*

Jason turns on the fireplace and kneels in his living room, intending to sit quietly. But almost immediately his mind races in a hundred directions. He watches his thoughts spin out and gently notes the content. "Thinking about my to-do list. Planning. Worrying." Then he brings his attention back to the moment—the warmth of the fireplace, the sounds of cars outside, the rise and fall of his breathing. With his eyes closed, he feels his body begin to settle, like a shaken snow globe coming to rest. As the frenzy of his mind clears, memories of old sins and conflicts begin to surface. He notices tension in his shoulders and the urge to stop.

Rather than give in, he continues to observe, with soft curiosity, what he is experiencing. From this quiet, grounded place within he watches, like floats in a parade, the thoughts and feelings that are going through him. He puts simple names on these floats: "Anger. Judgment. Memories." He returns his attention to the present moment. "Breathing in. Breathing out. Breathing in . . ." After about five minutes of cycling through distraction, noticing the distraction, and re-centering, he turns his intention for this time to inviting Heavenly Father into this moment with him. In his mind, he extends this invitation by opening a formal prayer, "Dear Heavenly Father, I'm grateful I have this time to be with Thee." He pauses and observes the sensations in his body and the thoughts in his mind. Rather than try to force them away, he brings these images and feelings to Heavenly Father in prayer, with simple descriptions, where they can be observed together. "Heavenly Father, I'm noticing anger. I'm noticing judgment. Images are going through my mind about what happened last year." He pauses. Breathing in. Breathing out. "Heavenly Father, now I'm noticing a peacefulness." Another pause. As his mind wanders to some unfinished email responses, he softly notes the wandering and returns his attention to this moment with Heavenly Father. For several minutes he sits in this space, observing with Heavenly Father the thoughts and sensations that arise, the distractions that pull him away from this moment, and the returning of his attention to being with God in prayer.

Lorna has a similar experience. Only a few verses in and her mind wanders, "Oh my, look at all those dishes. I really should've done those last night. I'm lazy. Amy's not lazy. I wish I was more like Amy . . ." Softly, she notices her thoughts have drifted. Rather than continue down that rabbit hole, she closes her eyes briefly, takes a deep breath, and escorts her attention back to this moment. Opening her eyes, she refocuses on the storyline in front of her. Before too long, she realizes she's skimming the words but she's been tuned out for the last half a page. She remembers her friend's advice: mindfully catching your attention when it has wandered is like getting a butterfly to land on your finger. You don't run around trying to grab it; you get calm, and it will come to you. She begins again, a few verses back. Each time her mind drifts, she notes but does not get stuck in the tangential thoughts, and then she returns her attention to the scriptures.

Things to Try

Bring patience, gentleness, and soft curiosity to moments when you find the mind scattered, agitated, noisy, overactive, racing, busy, apathetic, or unmotivated. Rather than trying to *make the discomfort stop,* try watching the details with compassion.

In anticipation of prayer or worship, experiment with ways to help settle and quiet the mind and body, like a shaken snow globe coming to rest. This can be as simple as taking a few moments to stop and notice the sensations of contact with the floor and the cool of air on your skin.

When you notice the mind wandering during a period of stillness, remind yourself that it's natural and normal for minds to wander, ebbing and flowing like the sea. Rather than trying to stop that rhythm, learn to work with the mind and train it over time. This can include:

- Tuning into the sensations in the breath or body—not *thinking* about them, but *directly* experiencing them.

- Gathering your attention around a single anchor (breath, body, scripture, God) to help steady the mind.
- When the mind wanders off again like a child in the grocery store, tenderly but firmly escort it back to your chosen anchor. When deeper struggles happen in your times of stillness, try bringing them into your circle of prayer—expressing as best you can the physical sensations in your body ("I'm noticing tearfulness" or "I feel a heaviness in my chest") or the thoughts going through your mind ("I'm noticing a lot of worrying thoughts about XYZ right now"). Rather than simply a distraction, this can help bring some of the most salient substance of your life into your communion with Heavenly Father.

CHAPTER 5

KNOWING:

Seeing Things as They Are

"The quieter you become, the more you can hear."

—BABA RAM DASS

THE PROBLEM: *Anastasia, a single mom of two teenage boys, stares at her closed scriptures as if they were a fortune cookie. If only the answers were tucked neatly inside on a little slip of paper, then cracking open the scriptures wouldn't seem so daunting. Last month her seventeen-year-old showed her a website questioning aspects of Church history that she'd never even heard about before. His normally happy demeanor has become more solemn as he has wrestled to reconcile this new information with his seedling testimony. Even though her faith is grounded in other ways, she wants to help, and she has been searching for the answers. "How do I help him 'get' what I already know to be true? How do I answer his questions?" she mumbled at the closed book in front of her.*

Overview

Recognizing thoughts as thoughts, rather than an indicator of reality or self, can provide assurance and clarity in the often-challenging journey of seeking to discern truth.

Rather than living by every thought that proceeds forth

out of our head, we can seek to increasingly live by every word that proceeds from God. As precious as we consider scripture, though, many of us fall into superficial relationships with these sacred words. It can thus become a rich practice to learn to *experience* God's words, rather than simply to let them pass through our minds.

Not-knowing is a defining feature of God's plan for progression in mortality—and not an aberration. If that is true, we don't need to be so rattled by not having all the answers, since walking by faith requires stepping into the darkness. This can help us create more gentle space to hold questions—for ourselves, for our families, and for our Church communities.

It takes maturity and strength to hold the complexity some questions invoke. Infusing an inquiry with more patience and openness allows both non-resolution and conviction to coexist.

If (and when) we hit resistance on the path to knowing, we can focus our intention on staying present with God, reminding ourselves that this is part of the process, and it will one day pass—for "now I know in part; but then shall I know even as also I am known" (1 Corinthians 13:12).

Questions about truth—how to discern it and how to hold onto it—can be the source of ongoing angst and deep pain. For some, this angst comes because they just don't have the assurances they wish for. Others are grappling for confirmation of truths learned, or have found new information that is disorienting and confuses truths once understood. For those wrestling to "know," or to absorb new knowing, there is one mindfulness teaching that can be a significant help.

Thoughts Are (Just) Thoughts

It is a human tendency to relate to whatever thoughts or ideas come to our mind as automatic reality—even more so, to the feelings that arise within. And no surprise! The landscape of our inner experiences is vivid enough that it's not hard to understand why we would assume those experiences are a reflection of *who we are* and the world around us.

But do we have to? The answer is no. An important part of mindfulness practice is growing awareness of the difference between what is *real* and what is *true*. The longer people are able to rest in stillness, the more a new, relieving discovery emerges: however real certain thoughts are, *not all* content passing through the mind is true, or good, or worth paying attention to at all! And with a little practice, we can come to relate to passing mental content as just that—rather than an automatic indicator of reality.

For some, it can help to imagine thoughts as a river passing by with you sitting on the bank, looking on. With children, you can help them imagine watching a "thought parade" safely from the sidewalk. Or you might imagine thoughts as clouds passing overhead, or as fireworks on the horizon . . . with you safely at a distance, just watching.

As soon as you push back from thoughts (and feelings, too), here's the best news: you don't have to take them so personally. Nor will you feel so driven by them. Instead of getting pushed, pulled, or consumed by a particular thought (or feeling), you can instead evaluate it with some objectivity: What is this thought? Is it worth anything? Is it true, or real, or good? Is it of God?

Then, you can make the call! If something is worth considering further, you can do so. If not, you can let it pass like the garbage truck that drives past your home every Tuesday.

One of our acquaintances experienced chronic depression, which made his mind vulnerable to harsh self-criticism. Initially he had interpreted these thoughts as shaming promptings from a disappointed God. This was complicated by the fact that the depression inhibited his ability to feel the joy of the Spirit—which seemed to confirm God's disapproval. With mindful practice, paired with guidance from people

"I find it difficult not to entertain the occasional negative thought!"

he trusted, he was slowly able to recognize that thoughts and feelings characterized by a harsh tone were *not* inspiration. Although this did not completely eliminate his harsh thoughts, it changed how he experienced them and helped him to not take them so personally.

This reflects precisely what is *so relieving* about this mindful realization: rather than feeling beholden to embrace every passing thought (or feeling)—including the garbage ones—as unquestioned reality, you now have another option. You can watch those thoughts (and feelings) and get in the habit of letting them pass right by (unless, that is, you want to hold onto something good or inspiring).

This is very different from what many of us are used to—and quite a contrast to many messages in the world around us: namely, that if you feel something, if you think it, well, it says something about you, and your life, and "your truth."

Experiencing God's Word

Rather than *living by every thought that proceeds forth out of our heads,* Christians seek to live "by every word that proceedeth out of the mouth of God" (Matthew 4:4).

That means making it a priority to spend time in texts we believe contain God's words and His will. But as important as scripture is to followers of Christ, the reality is, our time with these words is subject to the very same set of challenges we've explored in preceding chapters when it comes to prayer and Sabbath worship: wandering, noisy minds; an inner sense of drivenness to get-things-done; and outer distractions that can fill any bit of reading we attempt.

As a result, reading the scriptures—individually and even more so in a family group—can become a distracting, draining, even empty experience. And who in heaven's name (even with heaven's command) would want to keep doing that?

Like empty prayer or empty church worship, an impoverished practice of scripture reading can be easy to leave behind without sensing that we've lost much at all ("why waste time on something that's not doing anything for me?!"). Rather than simply walking away from scripture, however, what if we could recognize the way in which we are walking away from a *depleted experience* of scripture? And what would it take to more deeply, powerfully, intimately *experience* His words, rather than just letting some words occasionally pass over our minds?

Said another way, what would it look like to prioritize having an experience with God in the scriptures, rather than just *getting it done*?

The Mindful Practice Called Scripture Study

Reading a text presents a unique opportunity for another challenging but rewarding *mindful practice.* That may sound strange, especially given how accustomed we've been, all the way back to early training, to think of reading as largely about comprehension: *Hmmm, those letters mean "cat."*

Sacred reading involves more than simply identifying definitions of words, though; it's also *interpreting the meaning of those words*: what does that mean for me, here, *right now*?

And that's where all this starts to get *really* fun. It's one thing to understand what Isaiah's words meant for Babylon of his day, and another to consider their general meaning for our day. But it's *a whole other level* to find out what meaning God might want *you* to take away here and now—or, even better, to feel God's actual presence in inspired words that touch you.

No longer just you and a blank page, this is an encounter with God's words *and* God's own Spirit in this very moment of your life. Thus, as President Dallin H. Oaks taught, "We do not overstate the point when we say that the scriptures can be a Urim and Thummim to assist each of us to receive personal revelation."[1]

This is all quite different from the way we often speak of scripture—as if it is more like a chemistry textbook and our task is to figure out what everything means. This is more enjoyable than chemistry too!

To *deeply experience* God's word in this fashion, a little more stillness and silence can go a long way—along with *slowing down* enough to stay deeply present to the words. Joseph Smith was encouraged to "let the solemnities of eternity rest upon your minds" (D&C 43:34). And after five months in Liberty Jail, the Prophet himself reflected, "The things of God are of deep import; and time, and experience, and careful and ponderous and solemn thoughts can only find them out."[2]

Still feeling unsteady or unsure you're up to hearing God's voice in the scriptures? Here's where all that mindfulness guidance from previous chapters can help, such as: bringing back the wandering mind, accepting discomfort that arises, paying attention to what's going on in the body, and so on.

And when confusion arises, or you're just not sure you're understanding fully, that's not a problem either.

Not-Knowing as *Not* Scary?

Latter-day Saints recognize that, rather than an aberration in God's plan, *lack of knowing* is a central and defining feature of mortal experience.

Yes, it's somewhat counterintuitive that to become like God we have to leave His side in the cosmos and become ignorant infants, 100 percent dependent on other limited humans. How fascinating: to know as God knows, we must experience mortality through the tiny lens of our own subjective bodies and limited life context, without a clear view of our eternal past. But the reality is, in order to spiritually progress, we had to forget everything we knew in premortal life and dive intentionally, *knowingly* into a daunting embrace of *not-knowing.*

Rather than seeing this lack of certainty as a sign of failure, our faith community acknowledges this as *crucial context* within which our agency is preserved. In this world, "one is always provided with sufficient materials out of which to fashion a life of credible conviction or dismissive denial," Terryl and Fiona Givens note. The thing that "tip[s] the scale," they suggest, is the fact that each individual is "truly free to choose belief or skepticism, faith or faithfulness."[3]

In comparison, imagine if God made *crystal clear* His will to all humankind—whether they wanted it or not. That would change things, and not in a good way.

Remarkably, it's in the *lack* of clarity, the confusion, and the slow progression to knowing (from constantly changing states of not-knowing) that our growth and learning happen—and our freedom to direct our lives is preserved!

Making Space for *Not-Knowing*

If the gospel plan is not rattled by states of not-knowing, maybe we don't need to be either. Instead of having to "fight against" these moments, perhaps they can become platforms launching us into new inquiries and learning before our God.

A great deal of suffering might be allayed if we created more compassionate space to hold sincere questions, within ourselves and within our larger communities (family, ward, and stake). Individually and collectively we can "fear not" when faced with unresolved questions. Instead we can breathe deep. Relax. And get curious.

But oh, that space is not easy when we want to figure it all out, right? Are we *really* willing to wait—if that's what clarity requires? As ancient Chinese philosopher Lao Tzu writes, "Do you have the patience to wait till your mud settles and the water is clear? Can you remain unmoving till the right action arises by itself?"[4]

As challenging as it can be to not seem to be receiving anything back from God in prayer, Adam Miller proposes this as a pivotal moment: "When this happens, you'll have to make a choice. You'll have to decide whether to get up and leave the room or whether to continue in silence." If the latter, "You may discover that God's silence is not itself a rebuke but an invitation. The heavens aren't empty, they're quiet. And God, rather than turning you away, may be inviting you to share this silence with him. This is part of what atonement looks like: sitting in shared silence with God."[5]

One new mother who began to feel deep concern around the history of polygamy shared her concerns with her husband. Rather than try to "figure it out" and make it go away, they decided to create space around it and be patient. They chose to hold the questions in a sacred space and wait for further light and knowledge to come as they continued to look to the prophets and follow the Lord as best they knew how. When peace and understanding did come, although some questions still remained, the inquiry became more infused with assurance, patience, and a sense of God's love.

Another young man, trying to make sense of his sexuality and identity as he was confronted with feelings of attraction toward other men, wondered why God would allow him to experience something that "feels so natural" when those feelings seem to run counter to the family ideal that is taught in the Church. As challenging as it was to continue to trust in the teachings of Church leaders when cultural ideals and narratives were often so loudly critical of those teachings, he found some solace in the words of Elder D. Todd Christofferson, that "to declare the fundamental truths relative to marriage and family is not to overlook or diminish the sacrifices and successes of those for whom the ideal is not a present reality," and that "everyone has gifts [and]...can contribute to the unfolding of the divine plan in each generation." Elder Christofferson added that "much that is good, much that is essential—even sometimes all that is necessary for now—can be achieved in less than ideal circumstances."[6] This young man chose to trust that God would help him to understand the "why" of his experience in time, having faith that all of life's experiences are purposeful and have power to bring us closer to God. In the meantime, he would focus on living one day at a time, nurturing meaningful relationships with others and with the Savior, and serving in the kingdom in the best ways he could.

Even if not fully "fixed," faith struggles can be held in a mindful space with awareness and patience. No doubt, it takes maturity and strength to hold onto this complexity, and, for some issues, to hold them for a really long time. But rather than bearing such questions like some dirty secret we must take pains to hide from those around us (or hint that others do so), we can take confidence knowing that this is part of the process not just for some, but for *all of us.*

In this way, we can experiment with creating space where not-knowing can coexist quite naturally alongside conviction and passion. Perhaps it's the overemphasis of either that gets us mired.

Glorifying Uncertainty

More than simply "making space" for not-knowing, some have taken it several steps further, to the point of embracing uncertainty as a kind of ultimate aspiration. In this way, it can be tempting to glorify paradoxical confusion and uncertainty as somehow more enlightened—with "doubt" spoken of as a kind of higher state of consciousness. From this place, conviction itself can be portrayed as unhealthy or even foolish: "Don't be *too* convicted or certain." Some have even started pathologizing conviction as an inherent vice (aka "the sin of certainty").

As Latter-day Saint mindfulness teacher Thomas McConkie has put it, "*Unknowing* can be valorized in postmodern culture to the point that any form of knowing is branded as childish, or naive"—pointing out that "clinging to uncertainty is very much its own form of certainty."[7] Even those who claim "one cannot know anything," in other words, often do so with a lot of conviction.

More humility would go a long way for all of us, including among those who feel secure in their knowledge. As part of this, maybe we can all admit that discerning the truth of what's happening isn't always so easy.

Watching the Inner Workings

It's common to talk as Latter-day Saints about something like "feeling the Spirit" or "losing the companionship of the Spirit" as experiences that can (or should be) obvious. And to many people, *they may well be,* depending on where they are in their lives. But what about for those struggling in the middle of complex circumstances, or feeling overwhelming burdens, or undergoing extreme stress or acute trauma?

Very quickly, an experience that has the potential to be clear might get quite foggy and confusing—with the clarity of God's voice no longer so easy to discern. Rather than recognizing this, however, we have a tendency to lurch forward *insisting* we've heard God's voice. That leaves us vulnerable to uncritically accepting something that God might *desperately* want us to explore a bit more.

How can we be sure that our experiences involve God's true direction, rather than simply a conjuring of confirmation from our own ego? For starters, what if we took the time to observe our own inner workings more carefully?

Our experience is that this kind of space can help break down and pick apart the complexities of a thorny situation we're facing—including experiences that may feel otherwise scary or challenging. In this slowing down and intentional space, you see, we are allowing for something else to emerge: *insight.* That's why the most researched form of meditation is often called "insight meditation"—or what we might call "revelatory meditation."

As part of this inner watching, it's valuable to remember the powerful role that deeper emotions and convictions play in influencing what we see. It's not typically the heart that we think of when it comes to *knowing* something. And yet, the prophet-poet Isaiah writes about a people's failure to "understand with their heart" (Isaiah 6:10).

Or we might simply say, "Noah, you're not paying enough attention to how your emotions are influencing what you see!" As modern research by Dr. Jonathan Haidt and others has confirmed,[8] what we end up seeing, thinking, and believing is deeply influenced by our core convictions—often leading people to chase after beliefs that *match* their inner state. As much as modern humans love to believe that "logic" and "scientific facts" are driving their judgments, there's so much more going on! The Apostle Paul warned the early Saints about this in teaching that "the natural man receiveth not the things of the Spirit of God: for they are foolishness unto him: neither can he know them, because they are spiritually discerned" (1 Corinthians 2:14).

If our heart is dark, then, it influences our vision to see things in more of a dark light. And if our heart is light, we see things in a very different, brighter way. The key is to notice this—and recognize the influence, rather than just *living it out.* When we recognize our blind spots in being able to decipher truth (and we all have them), we are better able to navigate those vulnerabilities—and ensure that we move through our journey of learning with eyes wide open to all the many influences on what we see, think, and feel.

Then we'll be in a great place to truly *know for ourselves* the actuality of things.

Knowing by Direct Experience

After having communed directly with God, Adam and Eve were ushered into mortality to learn by *their own* experience. That's true for all of us—and it's a remarkable reflection of God's trust (and ours too) in the potential of this big, adventuresome plan.

But He doesn't leave us to stew and wonder alone. As the Saints bear witness to the world, a boy prophet spoke of meeting God directly, describing "a pillar of light . . . above the brightness of the sun, which descended gradually until it fell upon me" (Joseph Smith—History 1:16).

This expectation of divine teaching via raw, personal experience was shocking to many—and remains still foreign to many believers in today's world. But this is foundational to the Saints. Even while we anticipate our own experiences (one day) of personal, face-to-face communion with God, we look to prophets and seek as much of our own heart-to-heart communion as we can find here and now.

Suggesting more than an occasional heavenly hint, early Latter day Saint leaders have emphasized God's eager willingness to teach us as fast as we can receive Him. In Joseph Smith's Liberty Jail prayer, he writes, "What power shall stay the heavens? As well might man stretch forth his puny arm to stop the Missouri river in its decreed course, or to turn it up stream, as to hinder the Almighty from pouring down knowledge from heaven upon the heads of the Latter-day Saints" (D&C 121:33).

Is that how *you* see and experience God—and His willingness to teach? As Latter-day Saint mindfulness teacher John Kesler put it, "The Spirit is *right there*—just waiting for you to be open and present enough to receive His guidance, help and message of love and utter joy."[9] Attesting to this same radical willingness to teach, Joseph added on another occasion, "God hath not revealed anything to Joseph, but what he will make known unto the Twelve & even the least Saint may know all things *as fast as he is able to bear them.*"[10] It's fascinating to think that the Lord is as willing to teach the everyday Church member as He is to teach the prophet. The determining factor of whether or not we can be divinely tutored isn't our Church calling, or even whether we have lots of degree-endorsed initials after our name, it's *our capacity to receive* God's teaching!

President Russell M. Nelson similarly confirmed, "Oh, there is so much more that your Father in Heaven wants you to know."[11] As we create head and heart space to receive, and as we develop the strength to live what we are taught, the brilliance of eternities can be ours.

Knowing for Ourselves

Within this radically experiential orientation to knowledge, we Latter-day Saints also put words to our experiences—as all human beings do. In our case, we often translate raw experience into a set of propositions or beliefs, which we call "articles of faith" or, more simply, a "testimony."

It would be inaccurate, however, to describe a "testimony" as merely a set of intellectual propositions held to be true, since it's our own personal experience of God and His teachings that underlies these stated convictions.

In his own descriptions of truth, Joseph Smith said: "This is good doctrine. It tastes good. I can taste the principles of eternal life, and so can you. . . . You say honey is sweet, and so do I. I can also taste the spirit of eternal life. I know that it is good."[12]

Truth *tastes* good.

Joseph Smith also taught, "Reading the experience of others, or the revelation given to *them,* can never give *us* a comprehensive view of our condition and true relation to God"—hinting, on another occasion, "Could you gaze into heaven five minutes, you would know more than you would by reading all that ever was written on the subject."[13]

No wonder we focus so much on ordinances and direct communion in prayer! Despite this, we still sometimes live excessively in our heads. Thomas McConkie reflected on how often, instead of enjoying the richness of direct experience, we get satisfied with statements of belief *about* that experience:

> It's a bit like coming home from a wonderful vacation to Hawaii, telling your children what a magical place it is that you've just visited, then asking them to content themselves with the statement: "Hawaii is a beautiful place," rather than just going and seeing it for themselves! Rather than go directly to the experience of God's Majesty, we're often resigned to interacting with the symbols of the Divine in our minds, not realizing that we've lost the territory for a crummy map. It's as if we've traded an all-expense-paid vacation to paradise for a map of it, failing to understand that there's a difference between the two.

Thomas went on to explain how, five years into his own mindfulness practice, the restored gospel "came back to life" for him. "It wasn't just about symbols anymore, or credo. I had a distinct and direct experience that the symbols and language of the restoration were artifacts of *direct experience* of the Divine and that, in fact, we could make use of these 'artifacts' to reliably show us the way back to this celestial realm. Feed on mere words, and you're eating the husks of the Gospel; but understand the words as signs pointing to a Royal Banquet, and you'll never go hungry again."[14]

THE PRACTICE: *Anastasia, a single mom of two teenage boys, stares at her closed scriptures. She closes her eyes in prayer, "Father, I'm grateful my son's questions are providing an opportunity for him—and me—to come to know You even better. I love him, and I know You do too. Help me know how I can manifest this love as he seeks answers. I pray that this important wrestle he's having will be sanctifying. Help my patience and faith be strengthened. As I read today, soften my heart that I may see ideas in the words that will help my testimony, and my son's testimony, grow. I pray this experience of searching will strengthen our relationship to each other and to Thee." Finishing her prayer, she opens her scriptures to where she left off, 1 Nephi 15. Nephi is "grieved" that Laman and Lemuel are struggling to understand their father's teachings. "Oh, I can relate to this," she thinks, aware of the worrisome tension in her stomach. She reads on, "And it came to pass that after I had received strength I spake unto my brethren. . . . And they said: Behold, we cannot understand. . . ." Anastasia pauses and rereads the words, "after I had received strength." She takes a deep breath and ponders this phrase. Nephi's advice is to take time to receive her own strength before engaging her son in conversation. She feels a tearfulness in her eyes and warmth in her heart, a confirmation of the Spirit giving her permission to take the time she needs to reconnect with the source of her strength, the Savior Himself. She continues reading, "And I said unto them: Have ye inquired of the Lord?" She pauses again, noticing that this advice, to direct her son into prayer with the Lord, feels light, energizing, and right for this particular moment. She feels increased confidence that the Lord is aware of her son, and of her. She can feel that reassuring love soften the edges of her anxiety, creating the more patient, open mind-set her son has been needing from her.*

Things to Try

Practice approaching mental content in the mind as a *passing event*—a shuttle of thoughts—rather than an automatic reflection of reality or yourself. In this way, work to differentiate between what is *real* and what is *true*.

When you notice yourself "in your head" and consumed by analyzing and ruminating, practice consciously shifting attention to a broader observation of your full experience—body, mind, heart.

Begin to experience scripture time as a mindful practice of its own—bringing more silence and stillness into your reading, paying attention to sensations in the body along with feelings and thoughts that arise—all part of an ongoing interest in hearing God's voice in your own life.

When you notice a sense of craving or urgency for an answer to a particular question, observe what that drivenness feels like in the body, heart, and mind. Rather than demanding "answers," be honest with God about your own sense of urgency—while practicing gentleness and patience as best you can.

When the array of emotions, thoughts, and experiences gets tight, knotted, and confusing, rather than trying to "figure it out," make more tender space around the whole experience. Watch patiently until you can discern its distinct elements, noticing how emotions like anger, fear, or sorrow may be influencing what you see.

Being confronted with information we don't understand or didn't previously know can make us feel confused, tense, off balance—even lost. When you're confronted with the limits of your understanding, let your focus be on building your capacity to tolerate discomfort rather than on eliminating it—experimenting with ways to find stability underneath the confusion:

- Ease knee-jerk reactions of fear or stress, affirming that, *"It's okay that I'm thrown by this (or don't understand, or am feeling anger, or confusion, or hurt). I can hold complexity."*
- Bring to mind a difficult impression or thought that challenges you—noticing simultaneous sensations of imbalance, tension, or confusion in the body. Observe the motion and life of these sensations as they rise and fall and move from one physical spot to another.
- Practice *resting* in the underlying stability and calm of the awareness out of which you can hold and observe everything else, including the challenging thought. In that place of calm, learn to tolerate the mental tension

of not fully understanding while still maintaining focus on the Savior.

Periods of very intense not-knowing can go on for a while and be tiring. Give yourself breaks—times when you consciously put your questions down and focus attention on other things. This is not the same as avoiding through distraction or dropping out of the race altogether, but instead a conscious, mindful recognition that you're in a marathon, not a sprint. That means pacing, water breaks, and stretching are necessary to finish the race.

While creating internal space to patiently hold not-knowing, continue to simultaneously acknowledge the assurances you already have. Simple things like visual reminders of the core things you do know (pictures of Christ, meaningful quotes, music, and so on) can remind you not to forget about them as you expand your capacity to hold more complexity.

CHAPTER 6

BEING:

Eternal Life Right Now

"Forever is composed of nows."
—EMILY DICKINSON

THE PROBLEM: *Paula carried her potato casserole in through the back door of the stake building and headed toward the kitchen. The funeral was today. Out of the corner of her eye, she briefly noticed Sister Otis's family members gathering pictures on a table in the foyer in remembrance of their mother's long life. Scurrying into the kitchen, she set the dish down on the counter and looked for the Relief Society president to ask how to help. Since she wasn't around, Paula grabbed her phone and began scanning social media, only vaguely aware of her own rumbling hunger and the sounds of Sister Otis's family members in the hall. After a few minutes she looked up and mumbled, "Where's the Relief Society president?" Frustrated at the inconvenience of being bored when she was here to help, and aware of the other things pressing on her afternoon to-do list, she stuck the casserole in the fridge and decided to take off early instead—who would even really notice?*

Overview

When we trudge through the full sensory experience of our lives numb or on autopilot, the richness of little moments is sadly overlooked.

Living in the present moment integrates the body, mind, and spirit in a regenerating way—we feel so much more alive!

Living more "in the moment" isn't about indulging hedonistic pleasure. It's about experiencing the subtle details of our lives—both pleasant and unpleasant—and recognizing God's influence throughout.

Sometimes we get so caught up in other people's lives, or in representing our experiences online, that we miss out on relishing the richness of life unfolding here and now.

The Savior demonstrated a willingness to pause and be fully present with someone at uniquely inconvenient times. We can look for ways to practice this too.

Rather than simply anticipating being able to enjoy the sweetness of God's presence someday far into the future, we can deepen our connection to His peace, presence, and joy *now*—in this very moment.

Since heaven and eternity are not fairy tales to Christians, we admit: we *do* like to talk about them! This focus on life after death can, we also need to admit, sometimes take us away from relishing the goodness of *life after birth* . . . in the here and now.

Mindfulness teacher Thich Nhat Hanh taught that, compared to the miracle of walking on water, the more significant miracle is "to walk on earth," noting that "every day we are engaged in a miracle which we don't even recognize: a blue sky, white clouds, green leaves, the black, curious eyes of a child—our own two eyes. All is a miracle."

Treasuring the richness of the present moment is at the heart of mindfulness and contemplative practice everywhere. But for most of us, for different reasons, that's simply *not* our lived experience right now.

The Walking Mostly-Alive

People regularly come into our mindfulness classes so stressed out and worn down by life that they look and feel almost like zombies: emotionless, pale faces . . . hunched-over postures . . . permanent slight frowns.

Believers focus attention on the full separation of spirit and body in death (and the wondrous anticipation of resurrection), but far less attention goes toward ways that spirit and body can be estranged *in this life*. Various states of physical detachment can be triggered by sleep deprivation, physical illness, emotional illness, trauma (big or small), medical side effects, and high stress from overscheduled lives or relationship aggression. Illegal drug and porn use are also known to prompt states of dissociation.

As a result, the body, mind, and spirit can get significantly "out of sync," generating a semiconscious haze in which we can overlook so much around us.

Becoming (Even More) Alive

Given our human tendency to get caught up in a fragment of our experiences—"living in our heads," or "being consumed by our feelings," or "driven by our body"—there is gentle encouragement in mindfulness to expand our awareness to *all parts* of our experience, without overprioritizing any one element. In this way, we can break out of the tight compartmentalization of experience and open up to *all of our life,* moment by moment.

Over time, this can also help synchronize (or resynchronize) the body, mind, and spirit so that we are more fully integrated (aka alive!). Often, mundane and immediate experience helps us to start to recalibrate: a glimpse of tenderness, a belly laugh that shakes our whole body, or even a memory of past wholeness that gives us clues on how to rediscover it in the present.

As a child, for instance, Kyle spent hours upon hours every week (during the school year or not) in the forests of New England:

> *Those moments in God's garden were renewing and revelatory for me. As a child sitting on lichen-speckled granite boulders bathed in sunlight, I first heard God's voice of peace and love on the wind. I found my base, my calm on the glassy surfaces of sparkling riverways, paddling gently to minimize the ripples. The rustle and sway of the treetops matched the subtle rhythms of my settled breath. This was holy tranquility, the treasure of life. I was lucky to have had such a childhood and parents who valued experiences with nature (if only to keep four rowdy boys occupied). It was a beautiful life.*

Reawakening to the Abundant Life

When we've "grown up," of course, it's not always so easy to find the sweetness and fulness of life. It's interesting that when prophets describe the possibilities of a reinvigorated life, they use precisely the same language as they do in describing the literal Resurrection—being "made alive in Christ" (2 Nephi 25:25) and "alive unto God" (Romans 6:11)—*in this life.*

Other words used in contemplative cultures to describe this same deepening of life's richness, *awakening* or *waking up,* also have distinctively Christian meanings. Alongside the most obvious reference of the Resurrection, these words are used throughout scripture to refer to having spiritual eyes opened to be able to see the true nature of our relationship to God, rediscover the sweetness of following Him, and leave behind ugliness—as in the ancient prophet's plea to "awake, awake" and "put on strength" (Isaiah 51:9; 52:1).

Compared with the "sleepwalking" Elder Dieter F. Uchtdorf has warned against,[1] what would it mean for our whole lives to reflect this kind of vivid presence and life?

Truly Knowing What Is Here

In a well-known mindfulness exercise, participants start to experience this for themselves by taking ten to fifteen minutes to eat a single raisin. Five minutes into the raisin feast, wild new realizations, sensations, and observations have arisen—about something that, till that moment, had merited no particular attention.

If being fully saturated in a mundane experience can change a simple raisin moment, what about all the other moments of our day? A conversation, a person we pass on the street, the landscape on the horizon . . .

But what if that moment with that person (or the raisin) is quite unpleasant? Rather than trying to *insist* on enjoying something, as we sometimes do (*you* should *be feeling joy, you know*), how about just watching out for moments of sweetness in which we can immerse ourselves? As Elder Uchtdorf has taught, "No matter our circumstances, no matter our challenges or trials, there is something in each day to embrace and cherish. There is something in each day that can bring gratitude and joy if only we will see and appreciate it."[2] And on those days when it all feels truly miserable, we can expand our capacity to hold even that with wisdom and depth.

For example, a mother whose elementary school child died in a school shooting described how she related to her chronic, devastating grief. She didn't want it to consume her, nor could she eliminate or deny it. Instead she decided *to create a sacred space in her heart,* surrounded and contained by love, where that pain could be held and tenderly acknowledged.

In the midst of all circumstances, then, our faith can help us be more *here*—and not just run away. In reflecting on the closure of his religious abbey, one Catholic leader in Utah said, "I'm not threatened by the change." After describing how he leaves "yesterday to God's mercy," he spoke of moving forward in "what we call the 'sacrament of the now moment.'"[3]

Two Ways to Be in the Moment

When you start to speak of "living in the moment," don't be surprised if you get a few eyebrows raised in religious communities: *Hmm, kind of sounds like doing whatever you feel like, no matter the future consequences, right?*

That kind of "living in the moment" is not what we're talking about here. There is a difference between living *in* the moment and living *for* the moment. And what exactly we *seek* in that present (exclusively our pleasure or something more) creates two *very different kinds* of "living in the moment." One draws us to relish more deeply the richness of whatever is here in our own lives. The other tends to be a kind of hedonistic quest for pleasure, or to "feel good," and draws us to hungrily crave more and more of a certain kind of sensory experience or whatever richness we see in others' lives.

They are definitely not the same! Even while decrying hedonistic living, Elder Neal A. Maxwell taught, "We need to concentrate on what has been called 'the holy present,' for now is sacred. . . . The holy gift of life always takes the form of now."[4]

Engrossed in Someone Else's Life

One reason we end up missing so many moments in our own lives is that we are immersed in so many "more interesting, entertaining, and dramatic" lives calling for our attention all around us. Compared to That Guy Trying to Survive on the Island or That Girl Trying to Pick Her Dream Match, what's so special about normal ol' me?

Even when there *are* pleasant things we notice in our lives, sometimes we can be so preoccupied with "capturing" them for others that we consistently miss out on the richness of these moments ourselves. ("Oh, wait, hold on—I've *got* to get a picture of this to post online!")

Author Richard Rohr warns against "search[ing] for a life of more events, more situations which have to increasingly contain ever-higher

stimulation, more excitement, and more color, to add vital signs to our inherently bored and boring existence."

What happens if we intentionally pause all that seeking and activity? That kind of intentional stillness and silence, Rohr points out, can become "a portal to constantly deeper connection with whatever is in front of you"—thus revealing "the fullness of the now, instead of always waiting and wanting more, instead of waiting for the next thing, the more exciting thing, to happen."[5] This insight is something Ty found especially beneficial:

> *Something that has been particularly helpful to me in mindfulness practice is the emphasis on being in the present, surrendering stories and judgments about what "should" be, and allowing myself to live with a kind of compassionate awareness and acceptance for what "is"—right now. Even though my introduction to mindfulness was in the context of a secularized therapeutic intervention, something about it also felt so spiritually "right" and resonant, and the Lord taught me that this practice was key to my continued spiritual development and ultimately essential to my being sufficiently prepared for my later marriage. It transformed my*

relationship with myself and with God—increasing my capacity to trust in any path He might prepare for me, receiving "today's manna today" and letting God take care of "tomorrow's manna tomorrow." This also helped me understand the meaning of His prayer, "Give us this day our daily bread" (Matthew 6:11), and to more fully appreciate Alma's insight on how we "ought to be content with the things which the Lord hath allotted" (Alma 29:3) in this moment of time.

A Present-Focused Gospel

Relishing the present, of course, is not a foreign concept to Latter-day Saints. We just talk about it differently—focusing on "showing gratitude" and "recognizing God's hand in all things." Among other things, this kind of present-focused gospel helps us see the "same old" activities with fresh eyes, inviting us to find more richness in important, if repetitive, spiritual or family practices that may otherwise feel routine over time.

It's in relation to other people, though, that the true value of full presence really shines, as illustrated vividly in the Savior's own life. For example, when an important religious ruler's child is terribly ill, the large crowds follow Christ trying to make it to this child's bedside before anything tragic happens.

That's as intense as it gets: a prominent leader, a life-and-death situation with a small child, crowds watching, time ticking . . . no wonder the disciples were so focused on "getting there," into the future, to save this child. Most of us would also be totally preoccupied with what we were going to say and do in that future moment—not to mention with how these crowds, or this father, would respond if things didn't go well.

While no doubt experiencing the rush of these same human tendencies, Christ notices a sick woman in the street. But Christ doesn't simply see her; He is *so present* in the moment unfolding, right here, *now*, that He feels her silent touch on the hem of His garment. And stops.

"Can I call you back, Ed? I'm in the moment here."

He stops. The impending future crisis does not overwhelm His capacity to be totally present and ready to create a healing moment with this deserving woman (see Matthew 9:18–25; Luke 8:41–56).

How many moments do we miss—with kids, or spouses, or brothers and sisters at church, or even the same-old homeless lady on the street—because we're rushing forward with our own always-so-important tasks?

This magnificent moment in Christ's ministry also reminds us of how easy it is to get caught up in doing good things to a point that we overlook other opportunities or priorities. We get so busy that we forget about ministering to a neighbor in need, until we catch ourselves and refocus. As prayer or scripture reading fades, we notice and catch ourselves, exploring what happened before bringing our attention back to these priorities. We realize our mind is thinking about our to-do list rather than the sacrament, and we bring it back. We knowingly turn away from an indulgence contrary to God's will—but then we feel the inner angst, remember what we really want most, and come back to Him.

Whether in formal meditation or in our larger spiritual life, this rhythm of pausing and *bringing ourselves back* is core to both mindfulness and God's plan for us, not an aberration in either case.

Embodied Religion

Thankfully, each time we *come back* to our highest ideals and deepest commitments, we exercise a kind of muscle that grows in real ways, allowing us to embody and live out our beliefs and highest convictions.

A wonderful story demonstrating this living of our faith is when Brigham Young learned of the great suffering among people stuck in the Wyoming snow. He arose in general conference and declared: "I will now give this people the subject and the text of the Elders who may speak to-day and during the conference. It is this. On the 5th day of October, 1856, many of our brethren and sisters are on the plains with handcarts, and probably many are now seven hundred miles from this place, and they must be brought here, we must send assistance to them. *The text will be, 'to get them here.'*"[6]

Perhaps more than any moment in Latter-day Saint history, this sermonette embodies the practicality of "pure" lived religion at the heart of the Christian faith.

The message? Save My sheep. Feed them. Clothe them. Bind up their wounds. And cherish them as the brothers and sisters they verily are. For those of us interested in mindfulness, the message could continue: Don't just speak of being present (or philosophize about it). Go. Be. Present.

One Thing on the Schedule

Ever feel like you're missing out on the most important things in a day? You're not alone! Sister Sharon Eubank shared: "Sometimes I am so pressed with everything that I have to do that I don't even know what the priority is. I've started asking the Lord every morning when I wake up, 'What is one thing you want me to do today?'"[7]

This "just one thing" mentality can be refreshingly simple—and in different ways. Sometimes we like to say out loud in family planning sessions as a reminder, "We have only *one* thing to do tomorrow—*His will.* That's it." Although that *one thing* invariably includes lots of different pieces, it feels reassuring to remind ourselves what we're *really* trying to do and *why* we're trying to do it all.

When approached in this way, our lives can begin to flow out of our moment-by-moment responsiveness to God's will rather than complex configurations of competing loyalties to the day's various tasks. Catholic mindfulness teacher Thomas Keating similarly writes about scripture's emphasis "on listening and responding to the Spirit rather than initiating projects that God is expected to back up, even though God had little or nothing to do with them."

Even compared with whatever Big Exciting Plans we may have been trying to get God on board with, learning to rest in the adventure of seeking His will and receiving each moment with gratitude can open up a life far more exciting than any other glamorous alternative.

Eternal Life Now

In this same spirit, what if, rather than waiting for a distant future life, we could glimpse and experience eternal life *now?*

In 1836, at the very moment when Joseph Smith's ministry was unfolding in Ohio and Missouri, Henry David Thoreau began encouraging people to "find your eternity in each moment."[8] Jewish theologian Abraham Heschel also later encouraged people to "live the life of eternity within time."[9]

This idea is not unfamiliar to Latter-day Saints, who see glimpses of the glorious future of heaven in our own messy, day-to-day living here. Instead of an otherworldly, unrelatable, incomprehensible mystery, we understand this eternal life to be God's kind of life. "Rather than just measuring a life span," as Adam Miller puts it, "'eternal' names a certain *way* of being alive, a certain way of holding life as it passes from one moment to the next."[10]

This way of being alive involves, in part, seeing and relishing the divine in the routine, mundane details of life. As William Blake once said, "If the doors of perception were cleansed, everything would appear to man as it is, infinite."[11]

That doesn't mean we're aspiring for something mystical that departs from our current experience. On the question of what eternal life is like, Miller proposes: "It's like *this.* It's like now. . . . It is a certain way of doing whatever you're already doing. Eternal life is just like doing what you're doing right now, but doing it the way God himself would do it."[12]

That is the aspiration of the Saints. Instead of transporting ourselves *somewhere else,* we are on a mission to build heaven on earth—starting in our own lives and homes.

The Unsuspected Power of the Present Moment

For those around us who hear such talk as theological abstraction, it's worth reminding ourselves again of the wide span of positive consequences documented as arising from deeper levels of mindfulness. These range from a measurable decrease in various types of chronic physical pain, to a surprising relief that can come to those facing depression, anxiety, and eating disorders like anorexia and bulimia, to the cultivation of greater attentiveness for those who struggle to focus. There is even growing evidence that the cultivation of mindfulness, combined with other healthy activities, can literally change brain pathways.

Alongside all the effort to examine the objective health benefits of mindfulness, there has been relatively less attention given to exploring *why* present-moment awareness alleviates pain, in some cases so dramatically.

In one best-selling book on mindfulness for mental-health problems written by leading cognitive psychologists, for instance, they do not explain much *why* mindfulness can impact depression so substantially. Instead, they state in a kind of awe: "There is an *unsuspected power* in inhabiting the moment you're living in right now with full awareness."[13]

Could it be that Christians have the explanation that seems to be eluding other proponents of mindfulness?

Living in His Presence

Believers, once again, often speak of "meeting God" or "returning to His presence" as an event far off and distant—something distinctly separate from this life, something we look ahead to "one day" in the future.

While the literal face-to-face rendezvous with our Father is, indeed, something ahead of us, there is a stirring sense among Latter-day Saints of another kind of "meeting" that can perhaps take place much sooner—even right here and right now.

In a final talk of his reign, the ancient King Benjamin suggests remarkably to his people that God is "preserving you from day to day, by lending you breath, that ye may live and move and do according to your own will, and even supporting you from one moment to another" (Mosiah 2:21).

Did you hear that? Lending us breath so we can live and move, moment by moment. Does that sound like God is close to you?

For Saints, God is the Great I Am, not only the Great I Was or Will Be—a God who lives for us in the here and now.

In contrast, we have found that when our hearts are longing for the future or our minds are preoccupied with the past, we are also (almost automatically) quite distant from God. As soon as we recenter and connect again with the present details of our own experience—here and now—it's not uncommon to also find a renewed awareness of the God we worship: *the Great I Am with You Always.*

It's in this very (present) moment that God meets us. Could this be an explanation for the sweet and "unsuspected power of the present moment" experienced by so many in the secular mindfulness community?

Whatever the case, mindfulness can help remind us that a "return to His presence," in a very real and practical and daily sense, could be sooner than anticipated . . . as soon as the next breath.

THE PRACTICE: *Paula carried her potato casserole through the back door of the stake building and headed toward the kitchen. Out of the corner of her eye, she noticed Sister Otis's family members gathering pictures on a table in the foyer in remembrance of their mother's long life. She paused and watched as an older woman carrying a crumpled Kleenex bent down next to a small child in an oversized suit jacket, pointing at one of the pictures and whispering. Paula felt an empathic lump in her throat—she didn't know Sister Otis well, but she had attended her own grandmother's funeral last year, and the tender feelings she had that day came to her mind. She went into the kitchen, set the dish down on the counter, and looked for the Relief Society president. Since she wasn't around, Paula scanned the room and noticed a bouquet of bright yellow tulips sitting next to a dozen vases. Someone had started filling the vases but had apparently gotten interrupted. Jumping in to help, Paula breathed in the soft scent of the flowers as she filled each little glass vase with cool water, aware of the surprising heaviness of the vases contrasting with the delicate lightness of the tulips. She lingered in the delicious smells of the warming casseroles and noticed the early signs of being hungry herself. As she finished with the arrangements, she found her mind wandering to the other things pressing on her afternoon to-do list. Reminding herself that she had, indeed, blocked this time to be here, she brought her attention back to the moment: the cheery flowers, the image of the older woman and child, the muffled chatter in the foyer, the smells of the casseroles warming, the sound of someone playing quiet hymns on the organ. It felt good to be able to give to another ward family today, the way her grandmother's ward had served hers last year.*

The richness of this ordinary moment filled her with a sense of connection and peace.

Things to Try

When you find yourself going through the motions on zombie autopilot, pause long enough to notice the details of this ordinary moment, paying attention with childlike wonder to its various sounds, smells, colors, and textures. You might also try engaging all five senses, awakening your attention by listening, touching, looking, listening, and tasting something immediately around you.

Rather than trying to control, fix, or force a difficult or uncomfortable moment to be something different than it is, experiment with accepting things exactly as they already are, moment by moment.

Use the repetitive chores of the day to tune into the physical sensations they involve: showering, washing dishes, tidying up, walking from the parking lot into work, listening to music while folding laundry. These are all opportunities to practice being fully present in the glorious details of mundane activities.

When feeling overwhelmed by a disparate set of many tasks on your to-do list, experiment with reimagining this same day with "only one thing on your to-do list": God's will, whatever that is, moment by moment.

The next time you find yourself escaping into the fantasies of someone else's life, recognize what's happening. Pause enough to breathe, and take a look at the tender, precious life being neglected around you—resting your attention on its details enough to know what you are missing.

When you are numbing out or pushing away from the present moment (the urge to randomly look at your phone may be a cue), practice holding still, observing your inner reactions with curiosity and compassion.

Notice whether you are open enough to interruption by others needing your support and attention—whether they are loved ones, coworkers, neighbors, or strangers.

In meetings you run or tasks you're working on with others, sink into the moment a little more by consciously building in time and head space to just "be present" together.

CHAPTER 7

BEING TOGETHER:

Seeing as We Are Seen and Knowing as We Are Known

"When we are still, looking deeply, and touching the source of our true wisdom, we touch the . . . living Christ in ourselves and in each person we meet."

—THICH NHAT HANH

THE PROBLEM: *There was a reason people kept a little distance from Roger. He was not just quirky or weird, but a little off, sometimes saying funny things and almost always smelling a little. Guesses among people who knew him about which mental illness he had were a common occurrence. Roger had been baptized in his early twenties, and for the first time in his life he experienced some of the peace and happiness he had sought for so long. But he would be the first to admit that it wasn't always so easy to connect or relate. Most of the guys in the singles ward were so busy finishing college degrees or working that they had to protect their time, especially with someone like Roger, who they worried might get overly reliant on them. And sisters in the ward, although always kind, consistently deflected even slight efforts on his part to get to know them. One ward member, Sam, did spend some dedicated time working to help Roger see how some of his thinking patterns weren't accurate: "If you could only realize this, things would be a lot easier for you, man!" But when the advice didn't seem to have a big impact, Sam got discouraged and backed off. When Roger was admitted to the hospital again, it was a while before anyone in the ward realized he was gone.*

Overview

Meditators engaging in the "practice of mindfulness" and Saints engaging in "developing the pure love of Christ" are working toward a similar *way of being:* being loving.

Mindfulness is not about individual development alone, but also bringing individuals into deeper presence, connection, and intimacy with others.

In order to see the divine in one another, we can develop a greater spiritual capacity and gift to see each other more deeply. This helps us tolerate our own struggles and vulnerabilities as well as those of other people.

We must be careful not to reduce ourselves to mere "spiritual consumers." God is calling us to relate to one another in celestial ways—to go beyond viewing others by their appearance, the roles they play in our lives, or how they can be of use to us. Instead, we can seek to really see, hear, and be with one another.

A natural extension of being with one another deeply is an increased capacity to be a healing influence in one another's lives. Although compassion can be challenging because our instinct is to flee from or abolish suffering, by learning to "watch with" others in pain and "suffer with" them, we can grow in our capacity to minister as the Lord would.

Given our different weaknesses, gathering together for worship inevitably involves discomfort—which can be embraced not as a problem but as part of the process of growing and becoming a Zion people together.

Love by Any Other Name . . .

Mindfulness is often characterized as nonjudgmental, compassionate, and intentional presence with whatever or whoever arises in our field of awareness. Rather than a mere skill or technique, "practicing mindfulness" is about developing *a way of being*—even one that is aware, compassionate, wise, and understanding.

Sound familiar? Similar words are often used to describe *love*: nonjudgmental, compassionate, and wise, intentional presence with whatever or whoever shows up in our lives. Charity, or the pure love of Christ, is also something we understand as more of a *way of being,* than simply a feeling or emotion or a set of acts or alms.

In many ways, the Saints and the mindfulness community are using different language to describe a similar attribute—living as a loving being with our heart in the present. Indeed, Latter-day Saint author Robert Millet once defined love as "seeing someone truthfully."[1] Meditators engaging in the practice of mindfulness and Saints engaging in developing the pure love of Christ are, in essence, training similar, overlapping muscles.

Indeed, a central doctrine of the restored gospel is the nature and importance of relationships and community in our earthly as well as our eternal journey. Concepts integral to mindfulness are likewise not about individual development alone, but about bringing individuals into deeper presence, connection, and intimacy with others.

From the earliest events and revelations of the Restoration of the gospel, the Lord sought to prepare the Saints to build Zion—not only geographically but, even more, spiritually. Zion wasn't just a place, the Lord told them, but was "the pure in heart" (D&C 97:21). As much as the gospel was about being pure (*being* or *becoming* Zion as individuals), that purity also was intended to ripple outward into relationships and community to create a truly Zion people.

The value of caring for and ministering to one another is being appreciated at deeper levels within our community. In the Lord's initial revelation regarding the law of consecration (D&C 42)—what the early Saints called "The Law" and Lord would later refer to as "the law of the celestial kingdom" (D&C 105:5)—He implored the Saints to "remember the poor" (D&C 42:30), for in Zion there could be "no poor among them" (Moses 7:18). By seeking to draw their vision to something bigger than themselves, something of which they were a critical and interdependent part, the Lord reinforced a vision of the equal value of each of His children in the family of God and the need for us to care for one another.

Truth in the Face of the Other

Jewish philosopher Emmanuel Levinas taught that truth comes through the face of the other—hinting that if we pay close enough attention in the details of our interactions with each other, we can truly see what is happening and what is needed.[2]

It does take real time and space to notice these kinds of things, though. And let's admit it: Even when we are with others, talking with them, it's easy for interaction to revolve around banter about movies, sports, or weather. Can we see the sleepless nights in that face? The emotional desperation? The marriage unraveling?

A short time after the Lord's initial revelation to the Prophet Joseph regarding the law of consecration, Joseph was shown in vision the celestial kingdom. This revelation, known to early Latter-day Saints simply as "The Vision" (D&C 76), describes the essential quality of community and sociality among those who will be known as the Church of the Firstborn in the celestial world. In addition to receiving the fulness of God's light and truth and grace, this would be a community where "they see as they are seen, and know as they are known" (D&C 76:94).

What does that really mean? More than simply seeing as God sees, this refers to a quality of relationship that is deeply intimate: together being seen and known at a depth at which the Father Himself knows us. It's important to note that this quality of seeing and being seen, knowing and being known, is not just with our spouses or families—it's with the whole body of Christ, with all these relationships interwoven into the one great whole of our eternal family.

Mindfulness for Latter-day Saints is not simply about stillness or quieting down for the sake of being still, even being still for the sake of knowing God, though these are certainly part of it. It's also about slowing down and being still so we can be present with ourselves and with each other—to experience a deeper kind of intimacy with one another—to really *see* and *know* one another.

Beyond What Am I *Getting Out* of Church

In a Church-produced essay titled "Becoming Like God," it is noted that "Latter-day Saints tend to imagine . . . exaltation less through images of what they will *get* and more through the relationships they have now and how those relationships might be purified and elevated."[3]

It's easy for any of us, though, to end up focusing on what *we're getting out* of our every interaction at church. If we approach church with a shopper's attitude, then we may window-shop from the outside, looking around casually to see "what's in it for me?" *Is the Sunday School teacher up to snuff? No? I'll hang out in the hallway. Are there enough attractive people here who will be fun and entertaining, or is this a ward of oddballs and misfits? Hmmm, they look boring and uncool; I'm moving on.* As covenant people, however, we aren't *consuming* Zion, we are building and *becoming* Zion.

To become Zion, then, we must develop the capacity to look beyond outward appearances and truly see the divine in one another. Sister Virginia H. Pearce taught that the term *namaste*—a customary Hindu greeting—"means, roughly translated, 'I honor the Deity within you,'" which is "precisely what we do when we open our hearts to another; we honor the fact that he or she, like us, is a child of the same loving Father, worthy of all respect and careful attention."[4]

This is especially true when it comes to how we treat those who are different from our typical view of the "right" kind of Latter-day Saint. We must create a loving space for everyone in our pews and hearts, including that overperfumed, conservative old lady with the "Primary voice" and that tattooed, cigarette-smelling teenager who sings in a rock band. The story has been told of Sister Virginia Perry, whose husband, L. Tom Perry, was at the time president of the Boston Massachusetts Stake. One Sunday, she spotted a woman quietly settling into a back-row seat in sacrament meeting, arriving a few minutes late. Noticing the woman's T-shirt and jeans, Sister Perry sensed she wasn't sure she fit in, with everyone else wearing their Sunday best and sitting with their families. "So, Sister Perry left her family alone, went to the back pew, and asked the visitor if she would mind if she sat beside her. When the woman smiled in the affirmative, Sister Perry put her arm around her. The next Sunday Sister Perry came to church wearing Levi's and a T-shirt."[5]

How we interact with others in our ward is a living embodiment of the faith we profess. And to open our eyes and see those around us as "us," not "other," is a mindful skill of the heart. To then make the well-being of *us* a central focus is another beautiful practice.

Intimacy in Seeing and Being Seen

We are called to develop a spiritual capacity, a spiritual gift, to *see*—in particular, to see more deeply within one another. Folks in conservative religious cultures often use the term *intimacy* as a euphemism for sex, but we lose something essential when we foster in any way a connotation that intimacy is something inherently sexual or even romantic. The Latin root of the word *intimacy*, *intimus,* means "innermost," and the root of *intimus*, *interrus,* means "to go deeper." We experience intimacy, or "into me see," when we let others see our innermost selves—to be seen and known—and when we allow ourselves to fully see and know others. This is not a sexual or romantic concept—it's a universal human good wherein we learn to truly be with one another, to really *hear* one another. Mennonite minister David W.

Augsburger observed that "being heard is so close to being loved that for the average person, they are almost indistinguishable."[6]

We all need more practice in this. It's not uncommon for someone in a therapeutic setting to be brought to tears simply because they feel seen and heard in ways they've never allowed themselves to before. Ty had a client once tell him that he struggled even to get his family to simply hear and talk to him, to sit with him. Rather than being able to listen to what was going on in his heart, they wanted to fix him or offer solutions or give him a Church magazine article to read, when what he most needed was to feel like he was seen and valued even in his current wrestles.

In sum, if God is love—if love is the defining essence of His being—and our call is to become more like God, it is our birthright to become love as well. But how do we become love? We practice it by being in relationships that challenge our capacity to love.

How is this to happen, though, if we're always focused on looking our best and not showing too much weakness or struggle? It is truly being honest about where we are that allows us to learn to love each other as God is asking—not only to see and know and love others, but to allow ourselves to be seen and known and loved. Christian writer

Timothy Keller noted: "To be loved but not known is comforting but superficial. To be known and not loved is our greatest fear. But to be fully known and truly loved is, well, a lot like being loved by God. It is what we need more than anything. It liberates us from pretense, humbles us out of our self-righteousness, and fortifies us for any difficulty life can throw at us."[7]

Healing Together

A natural extension of our ability to be with one another, to experience deeper intimacy and connection with one another, is a greater capacity to be a healing influence in one another's lives. In an address to young adults, Elder Jeffrey R. Holland made a specific request for healing: "healing for others, healing for those you love and, yes, perhaps especially for those you don't. The people around us need a lot of help, and I think the Lord expects us to join in that effort. I think that is what he meant when he said, 'Come; see what I do and watch how I spend my time.'"

He continued: "We all know that wonderful call for more labourers into the work of the harvest refers primarily to teaching and testifying. . . . But I wish to suggest tonight that in context it surely is a call to heal one another as well. . . . I ask you to be a healer, be a helper, be someone who joins in the work of Christ in lifting burdens, in making the load lighter, in making things better."[8]

As part of our baptismal covenant with Heavenly Father, we commit to be one with Christ, including being part of His people. We are invited "to bear one another's burdens . . . to mourn with those that mourn . . . and comfort those that stand in need of comfort" (Mosiah 18:8–9).

There's a Hebrew phrase, *tikkun olam,* that means "healing the world" or "repairing the world," which in Judaism suggests an idea of humanity's shared responsibility to heal, repair, and transform the world. It speaks of our responsibility to be partners with God in completing His vision for the world so His presence can be fully revealed.

As we invite the healing work of Christ into our lives, He then invites us to be a healing presence in the lives of others.

Watch with Me

In order to be a healing presence for others, we need to first truly *be there*—sitting with them, feeling their hearts, truly *being with* them. One of the greatest gifts we can offer people is to be in their lives in a lifting, healing way—even and especially when they are hurting the most.

The term *compassion* comes from the Latin *com-passion,* or "to suffer with." We can't truly minister to one another unless we can have true compassion for one another, a capacity to "suffer with" one another. Catholic priest and writer Henri Nouwen recognized the challenge of turning toward another's pain when he taught: "Let us not underestimate how hard it is to be compassionate. Compassion is hard because it requires the inner disposition to go with others to the place where they are weak, vulnerable, lonely, and broken. But this is not our spontaneous response to suffering. What we desire most is to do away with suffering by fleeing from it or finding a quick cure for it. . . . And so, we ignore our greatest gift, which is our ability to enter into solidarity with those who suffer. Those who can sit in silence with their fellow man, not knowing what to say but knowing that they should be there, can bring new life in a dying heart."[9]

During one ministering visit to a sister in his ward who struggled with depression, Jacob made some humorous remarks in an attempt to lighten the atmosphere. At one point, the sister interjected, "Please stop, Jacob. I don't need you to distract me from this or make it go away. I just need you to *be here* with me."

Similarly, in long battles with cancer, Jacob's mother and brother each remarked on how nervous it made some to be in their presence. People often tried to steer conversation away from what was happening, almost needing the distraction. In some cases, his mother and brother felt as if *they* needed to comfort those visiting. Jacob recalls:

> *On one occasion, though, I'll never forget our bishop arriving at the hospital and walking quietly, straight to Sam's bed. Without so much as a greeting for anyone else in the room, the bishop felt prompted to hold his hands in his own, and, looking directly into his eyes, he said, "Oh, have we been praying for you! How are you doing?"*
>
> *Deep comfort came in an excruciating moment. I weep even today to think about witnessing that encounter, watching a servant of the Lord doing just what my brother needed in that moment.*

No distraction. No platitudes. Just being there.

In the Savior's own worst moment, what did He ask of those closest to Him?

"Tarry ye here, and watch with me" (Matthew 26:38).

Just stay close . . . don't leave me alone.

If that was what Christ Himself needed, how about the many hurting around us? Are we willing to do that, even if it *hurts us* a little?

Coming Together to Be (Un)comfortable?

It's common for us to talk about the aim of Church gatherings to be uplifting, comforting, and consoling our spirits. Although these are things we all understandably want, what happens when the opposite happens, and it's *hard* to be with others? Is that *even okay*?

The story is told of a community of monks living together well on an isolated mountain, until one monk began seriously annoying everyone else. Finally, in the middle of a fight, that monk stormed off and moved out of the monastery, much to everyone's relief. The head monk, however, went and convinced him to come back. The other monks were appalled, asking, "Why did you do this? We just got rid of him!" The wise monk responded, "We need him. He is the yeast to our bread. Without him, we will not grow."

Are we open to *other* kinds of "leaven" in the loaf? One Sunday, while serving as Primary president, Carrie was not at her best at church:

> *I dropped important balls, put my foot in my mouth, and was all-around clumsy in my interactions with others. I retreated home, and, right in the middle of my sulking soirée, had an awful epiphany: I* am *the yeasty monk! I am the yeast monk in Primary!*
>
> *That led to a full-on weeping and wailing session, which my wise husband just sat and watched, in awe, probably, at my drama. I went on and on about how I'm not a good leader . . . and someone seriously needs to fire me . . . and how we need to have paid clergy so they don't have to deal with my mess-ups. . . .*
>
> *Why am I being asked to subject others to my weaknesses? How does this really benefit anyone? Why do we have to worship as a group like this?*

Christian author John Backman has written that his motivation to come to church is, in part, *so he can be uncomfortable*. Compared to staying home in his own thoughts, he describes how worship in a collective body allows him to be challenged by others' ideas that sometimes even drive him nuts![10] How easy it would be to be united if we simply agreed on everything, right? How valuable, then, it is that we *do not agree* on so many topics—politics, health, Napoleon Dynamite—and are *still* asked by the Lord to be one and learn to be united.

These words from Thich Nhat Hanh, a Buddhist monk, are a helpful summation, translated into language more representative of a Latter-day Saint community:

> In the ward (*sangha*) there must be difficult people. These difficult people are a good thing for you—they will test your capacity to build Zion and practice Christlike love (of *sangha* building and practicing). One day when that person

> says something that is not very nice to you, you'll be able to smile and it won't make you suffer at all. I am speaking to you out of my experience. I now have a lot more patience and compassion, and because I have more patience and compassion, my happiness has grown much greater. You suffer because your understanding and compassion are not yet large enough to embrace difficult people, but with practice you will grow, your heart will grow, your understanding and compassion will grow. And thanks to the ward (*sangha*) practicing together, those people will transform. That is a great success.

It's the caring about each other that turns a ward into a covenant people. And that means loving those who are quirky, frustrating, or downright "out there." Because the reality for every single one of us is, well, some days you're the bread, and some days you're the yeast. And we all need each other to keep growing.

THE PRACTICE: *There was a reason people kept a little distance from Roger. It's not always so easy to know how to respond to someone facing significant mental or emotional challenges. And although people in the singles ward did their best to help him know he was welcome, there were a lot of genuine questions. After counseling together about how to help Roger, some of the ward leaders felt a prompting to encourage a few in the ward to try to get to know him more personally. Given the legitimate concerns some sisters had about being alone with him, the Relief Society president, Wendy, arranged a surprise party on his birthday focused on celebrating his life. And following what his elders quorum president had privately encouraged, Sam decided to bypass more advice to try to help Roger, and instead start to ask some honest questions he was curious about: "So, what was your family like growing up, man?"*

"Not sure I want to talk about that," Roger said abruptly. "No worries . . ." Sam responded, before Roger quickly added, "lots of bad

memories. Got beat up more times than I remember. And Dad would always make sure to tell me how worthless I was anytime he got even a little mad. The worst was seeing what he did to Mom."

Sam waited as Roger paused and closed his eyes. He couldn't imagine what that had been like, thinking for a moment about his own adoring parents. As Sam felt emotion start to rise in his chest, he reached out and touched Roger's shoulder, noticing a tear rolling down his big cheek: "Nobody's really asked me about that for a long time, Sam. Thanks. Hope it doesn't scare you away."

"Not at all, brother. I'm amazed at where you are today. Your testimony the other day was beautiful. I'm in no rush . . . this is important. So, what was that like going through all that as a young child? And would you tell me more about what happened next—and how you went from that kind of pain to the life you have today?"

Things to Try

Notice stories or labels you carry around for different people, and how they can inadvertently establish all "manner of -ites" (4 Nephi 1:17): "druggies," "Utah Mormons," "inactives," "married too young," "geeky," "Why is s/he single?" How do these assumptions affect your interactions or feelings toward these "others," particularly your desire to serve and love them?

When someone is making choices that are scary or hard for you, practice sitting with your discomfort. With the Lord's help, find compassion in your heart for them—doing your best to meet them where they are—and seek understanding from a place of interest and kindness.

When you notice hard feelings for someone, practice tolerating the discomfort of going outside your comfort zone by extending kindness to them. If not in their presence, try this on your own:

- Bring to mind the name and image of that person.

- Remind yourself that the Lord loves them and the universe is made for them, too.
- Wish upon them in prayer all the love, goodness, comfort, and freedom Christ offers them.
- Repeat.

When in the presence of someone suffering, notice what is going on inside for you—watching the tendency to distract or want to push away. As best you can, practice "watching with them" in as much presence as you can bring. While staying open to ways to alleviate their suffering, let yourself really *just be with them*, too.

Recognize that really showing up in our relationships, authentically and lovingly, takes emotional effort and time. Just because that feels hard or inconvenient doesn't mean you're doing something wrong. Be patient with yourself and schedule meaningful respite with the Savior Himself, to recharge and keep perspective.

While mindful relational intimacy is about being whole, real, and sincere, it is not synonymous with inappropriate self-disclosure. Authentic presence requires an awareness of context and includes maintaining healthy physical and emotional boundaries.

Next time you reach out to minister to a neighbor or family member, watch the tendency to *get through* the encounter or "get done" with it. Experiment with letting yourself forget the clock a little so you can immerse yourself more in the moment.

When discomfort arises in interactions at Church or home, breathe deeply and practice accepting this as an inherent part of building a Zion community—together!

CHAPTER 8

BECOMING:
Eternal Progression, Moment by Moment

"Try a little harder to be a little better."
—PRESIDENT GORDON B. HINCKLEY

THE PROBLEM: *Jarom and his fifteen-year-old daughter, Anja, were scanning the example list of goals the Church had provided for youth. "Which do you want to do?" he asked. Anja was engaged, but unsure, "Uhh, I don't know . . ." She pulled the list closer. "This one looks easy, how about that?" she said, pointing to the line, "Memorize a hymn." "Oh yeah," he nodded, "we can get that one checked off quick. What else looks easy?" She scanned again, "Maybe something with exercising?" "Nah," he frowned. "You've got so much going on with homework and violin—isn't there anything with instruments? That way you could count what you're already doing and still get credit." She shrugged. "Sure, that's fine. Are we done, then?" she mumbled, reaching toward her phone.*

Overview

Rather than an unrelenting burden of striving, progression can be experienced as a constant excitement of endless expansion. So many of the precise details of earth life converge to allow a unique and ongoing adventure of choosing and becoming.

Growth and learning can be pursued in a gentle and deeply patient way that reduces stress and suffering. Handling and pushing ourselves (and others) roughly toward progress is anti-Christian.

Goals and plans can be approached as meditations on unfolding hopes and intentions rather than something to merely get done.

Mindful growth begins with powerful acceptance, grounded in the love of God for us *right now*—in the middle of our messes. Mindful presence helps us stay calm and less reactive, thus increasing our agency to make choices in line with our core values.

Acceptance is not the same as resigning oneself to challenging conditions forever. Rather, it is to be here and now, in a calm and wise way, enough to know what to do next.

Stillness is not the enemy of seeking. It is not an escape from reality, duty, or action, either. Any opportunity for contemplation can help settle our hearts and ground our decisions in a deeper wisdom—thus increasing our power and effectiveness.

There is nothing more quintessential to Latter-day Saint life than learning, growing, and what is affectionately called "eternal progression."

But for some, this whole idea is not so lovable. It can end up feeling quite wearying, as if we're being asked to strive constantly for someplace else and remain endlessly dissatisfied with the here and now. Surely, some conclude, this is the direct opposite of mindfulness and its full acceptance of the present . . . right?

Not quite.

"I'll give it to you straight, Benson. We don't think you're maximizing your potential."

Presence *vs.* Progressing?

It's understandable why the idea of eternal progression can seem in contradiction with the core of mindfulness—as if our attention to future possibilities requires an unwillingness to embrace the present moment while we always aspire for something better.

It's also true that a constant sense of not being enough, not doing enough, and always having to do more can feel like being stuck on an endless hamster wheel. That can be truly draining and exhausting for any of us.

If there are so many benefits from embracing things as they are, then should we maybe not fuss so much about looking into how things could be any different? That's where many seem to end up. But they *don't have to*—because our aspirations toward heavenly things simply don't require us to be constantly, naggingly dissatisfied with the present moment. We can get away from a pressure-filled, stressed-out, self-loathing approach to growth and progress without abandoning the idea of progress and growth altogether.

Growth is an inescapable part of mindfulness practice. And there is nothing that says the pursuit of profound change on the pathway of eternal progression cannot also be experienced as compassionate, spacious, grace-filled, and shot through with love . . . in another word, *mindful.* We believe that is just as Christ would intend it.

What people sometimes miss is that there are *very different* ways to approach growth and progress. If that is true, maybe we need to get clearer on what those differences are. For instance, is our desire for change fueled by a mind-set of self-loathing, people pleasing, and frantic pressure, or by the love and grace of God?

In what follows, we revisit several ways to ensure that our approach to progress and growth is sufficiently compassionate—drawing us along to new adjustments and fresh possibilities, moment by moment, with patience and compassion.

Becoming Gently

In contrast to the wildly popular messages of self-acceptance and personal discovery in the world today, Christ and His prophets continue to raise an uncomfortable proposition: God wants to *change us,* making us far more than we can possibly comprehend.

Even though Alma rightfully calls this a *mighty* change, it would be a mistake to see it as an aggressive transformation. Handling and pushing ourselves and others roughly toward "progress" is anti-Christian. And Christ's is not a gospel in which the ends justify the means—quite the opposite!

How often do our perceptions of God still conjure up the image of a kind of harsh drill sergeant itching to give out more marching orders? For example, the joke, "Don't pray for humility or you'll get it!" perpetuates the impression that getting closer to God invariably means He will allow or inflict painful "learning." One sister we know had been reflecing on specific inspiration she had received about personal changes she sensed were needed in her life. When this guidance first came, however, she interpreted it as slightly shaming "marching orders from God, as in 'Here's what you need to learn! Here's what you need to do to fix yourself!'" This woman continued:

> As I spoke with a kind, wise friend, she confirmed that the lessons and direction did indeed seem very relevant and important, but, she clarified, "I don't think God's really barking orders at you. You make it sound like He can't stand you as you are. Like He's frustrated with you and anxious for you to change. I think He's giving you this guidance because He's showing you how to heal the wounds that are creating this problem for you." In that moment I saw God in an entirely different way: "He's not scolding me, He's healing me! He's not motivated by judgment. He's motivated by love."

Unlike many earthly parents, the God we worship, though earnestly interested in the growth of His children into their full stature, encourages that progress "without compulsory means" (D&C 121:46).

We too can pursue growth in our own lives without so much force—what one mindfulness teacher calls "the subtle aggression of self-improvement."[1] Rather than trying to become something completely different than we ever have been previously, this is about a radical restoration to who *we really are* as literal children of Heavenly Parents—in the words of Jesus's most famous parable, "coming to ourselves" (see Luke 15:17).

In contrast to that popular notion of simply "celebrating who you are," this involves an often difficult, iterative process of learning, yielding, sacrificing, and growing into a bigger identity than we can grasp right now. Rather than something to simply get efficiently accomplished, "becoming" is an ongoing aspiration of disciples. As President Dallin H. Oaks observed: "The Final Judgment is not just an evaluation of a sum total of . . . acts—what we have *done.* It is an acknowledgment of the final effect of our acts and thoughts—what we have *become.*"[2]

This is not an optional path if we are to take the words of Jesus seriously. Christ insists that without this kind of fundamental change in our hearts and minds, we simply cannot "enter" or "inherit" the kingdom of God. However, unlike being barred from Disneyland or turned away from a country's border, those who have not reached in this direction *will not want* to be in this new place.

Even so, our reaching for this kind of change can sometimes turn into a problem.

Embracing Patience

It's popular among coaches to emphasize to athletes the need to be *discontent,* "never satisfied." While this may get results on the field, how well does that work for us in real life?

Not so great. What would it mean to be more accepting and present in whatever stage of growth we are currently in? As Joseph Smith taught, "When you climb up a ladder, you must begin at the bottom, and ascend step by step, until you arrive at the top; and so it is with the principles of the Gospel."[3] After noting our God-given capacity for expansion as we aspire to return to our heavenly home, the Prophet added poignantly, "But we consider that this is a station to which no man ever arrived in a moment."[4]

Can you feel right now the relief that a little more patience might bring to your own life?

As Elder Dieter F. Uchtdorf has noted, we can "even wear our busyness as a badge of honor, as though being busy, by itself, was an accomplishment or sign of a superior life."[5]

Compare that to seeing a group of children playing—perhaps happily keeping a balloon afloat off the ground. Even amidst our goals and plans, that may be a mood we can adopt to recharge and regain the lightness of our lives and rest our being in the joy of the moment.

Accepting Discomfort

When challenge and discomfort come, there's one thing many of us fall into that makes the pain far worse. Even without being fully conscious of it, many of us decide that we're *not okay* with things that are uncomfortable, too hard, or boring in our spiritual practices or even our family relationships. Let's get rid of boring; that's not pleasant. And while we're at it, let's nix any irritation, confusion, or hurt feelings. That's all getting in the way of the loveliness we're *supposed* to be feeling in our relationships and worship, right?

Of course, we realize this isn't how it really works. Becoming like our Heavenly Parents, becoming a family, becoming a ward, takes discipline and stretching. That's why it all takes patience, along with some challenging practice.

For many of us in society today, our awareness of our emotions goes little beyond "feeling good" or "feeling bad." But "good" and "bad" are not feelings, they're judgments. What we typically mean is that the "good" ones are the feelings we like, and the "bad" feelings are the ones we don't like—which means we will typically do what we can to avoid the latter while we chase after the former. But someone can just as easily feel "good" (at least temporarily) doing something unhealthy or destructive, and feel "bad" having experienced something very normal, such as a significant loss.

So rather than automatically pushing away uncomfortable feelings or grasping after pleasant ones, we can begin to practice something else: stepping back and observing what is happening—with more openness and less immediate judgment. From that place, we can consider how every emotion can teach us something—even the ones we don't like: sadness, fear, anger, and so on. But it becomes pretty hard to learn from our feelings if we can't be with them in a stance of openness.

This is important to understand, because if we can't be with our own difficult feelings or experiences or pain, we're going to find it extremely tough to be with the hard emotions of others.

Moving Forward by Stopping

To be present and accepting *here and now* is not the same as resigning oneself to current conditions forever. Rather, it is to *be here and now* with calm and wisdom, enough to know what to do next. In his famous "House Divided" speech, Abraham Lincoln also said, "If we could first know where we are, and whither we are tending, we could better judge what to do, and how to do it."[6]

Instead of opposing progress, then, these moments of stillness and sitting can become an integral part of developing the divine characteristics we are trying to embody.

That's quite different from the kind of progress and striving so evident in the larger world around us—a style that is driven, consuming, and always grasping for more. To those accustomed to this approach, stillness can thus be mistaken as not only a lazy activity but the utter abandonment of industry, interest, and commitment to betterment.

That may be why it's so common to find ourselves battling with these feelings when we attempt to come to stillness.

Stillness can help us *turn toward* and acknowledge what is really going on, as well as open us in profound ways to new questions about other possible steps. It is an attempt at more fully opening the soul to revelation and learning, and to hearing those voices often ignored.

Given our tendencies toward snap judgments and automatic assumptions, stopping also allows us to consider the meaning we are assigning to experiences and to explore which interpretation—among many—feels right.

Rather than just *getting along* to where we want to go, this ultimately means *being here* first. The question of *what next* then becomes quite an adventure.

In all these ways, stillness is not the enemy of active seeking, nor is it an escape from reality, duty, or action. It adds perspective to our activity. It provides information that improves our seeking. Stopping to be still makes whatever desires we then pursue better—more productive, meaningful, and satisfying.

Appreciating Our Aspiration for More

Could some of our desire to be more than we currently are perhaps be a result of our own ancient experiences? Could it be that we have deep, visceral memories of a Father and Mother who we *witnessed* having all power and all knowledge—able to do remarkable and miraculous things?

If so, what would it mean to become *more accepting* of those deeper impulses for more—and to bring more compassionate attention to them? By contrast, when we are only vaguely aware of the inner discrepancy between our expectations and the life we are living, this dissonance can quickly spill over in anger, frustration, or bitterness about life.

In other words, maybe it would help to recognize more consciously the Christian fact that we *are* foreigners (aka immigrants, refugees) in this world. No surprise, then, that we may not always "fit" or be "comfortable." And no wonder that our expectations and hopes can so often seem outsized and poorly fitting in this world, as would be natural, of course, for all *supernatural* plans.

Rather than constantly telling ourselves we're "never going to be perfect," and trying to "accept that we can only do so much," maybe it's time for us to also recognize this dissonance as a *witness of who we really are.*

Mindful Planning and Goals

As we reach for new growth, it's only natural to come up with different goals and plans to guide us along—all valuable practices. Once a certain plan or goal is set, however, it's not uncommon for people to become so consumed with achieving it that they lose touch with the inspiration behind it—perhaps missing out on some of the full benefits as well.

When Carrie recently felt some personal prompting in prayers to focus more on "building community," she quickly found herself pestering God for a "to-do" item that she could check off her list.

> *I kept asking, "Okay, but what am I supposed to do? Should I have people over for dinner? Do I need to say hi to more people at church? Do I send thank-you cards to the sacrament meeting speakers? What do you want me to do here?" But the impression I received back was something like, "Sure, you can do any of those things, but you're missing the point."*
>
> *I realized that God wasn't asking me to complete a task, He was asking me to change my mind-set. To (gasp) evolve as a human being. So I started approaching "build community" less as a task and more as an ongoing meditation—holding this intention in my day-to-day awareness with an attitude of openness to further revelation or inspiration that may unfold in the moment. I found myself asking, with soft receptivity, "Ahh . . . here I am in this moment (in the hall at church, in choir, talking to my sister on the phone, organizing the chairs for the Primary room). What options are yet unseen or could unfold organically to 'build community' in this moment?" And then I would consciously tune into the Spirit for inspiration in that particular situation. I came to realize that learning how to tune into revelation and be an instrument for God seemed to be the bigger objective, not just completing a set of tasks.*

Although not as cut-and-dried as just *getting something accomplished,* how much more exciting it is to approach goals and plans from a more mindful place—allowing God to lead us, moment by moment, in this lively process of becoming.

This Adventure Called Earth Life

Latter-day Saint scholar Randall Paul reflects on how remarkable it is to consider God's willingness to create unique mortal conditions that involve "erasing our memories" (thus obscuring the true purpose of life, as well as God's own reality) while allowing us to be subject to fear, starvation, and death. "How could that be seen as any sort of reasonable test?" he asks rhetorically.

The Latter-day Saint answer is that it's *so important* that we retain space for authentic choice that the whole design of mortality centered on it! This includes many of the fuzzy, confusing, uncertain, vague aspects of life that can drive us nuts (especially if we're not appreciating their purpose or value).

Consider what would happen if we *didn't* forget anything that had happened—eons ago, or even days ago. In what ways would that constrain or overly shape our choices today? And how would it be to have *perfect clarity* as to the truth and reality of things—no confusion at all? In what ways might that be a serious damper on our freedom to chart our own path forward?

In a remarkable way, all that lack of clarity, confusion, and forgetting *preserves space* for this marvelous adventure of mortal freedom. If future possibilities of eternal life really are *so good* that they would overwhelm us, then better make sure that human eyes *do not see*—nor ears *hear them,* right? Otherwise, how could we ever choose otherwise?

As Terryl and Fiona Givens write, "An overwhelming preponderance of evidence on either side would make our choice as meaningless as would a loaded gun pointed at our heads"—with a genuine option to believe (or not) required to be "perched precariously between sets of demands held in dynamic tension."[7]

Even the natural forgetting that happens along the way allows each day to become like a "mini-veil"—a forgetting that requires us to recalibrate and really dig deep in what we want.

Given this carefully designed setup, we are met with a mind-boggling array of choices each day. And an incredible test over a lifetime!

As hard as it can be to make mistakes and endlessly learn for ourselves, Adam Miller writes: "You have no choice but to learn as you go. . . . You are a pioneer. Life has never before been lived in your body. Everything must be done again, as if for the first time. You are an aboriginal Adam, a primal Eve."[8]

Becoming Ourselves, Moment by Moment

Any such choice, from a Christian perspective, causes numerous rippling effects in different directions—changing our mind and heart in tangible ways. We reject this, seek that, yield to this, go after that . . . and our heart keeps getting reshaped.

Simultaneously, our light keeps growing (or fading) as our awareness keeps expanding (or contracting). As Joseph Smith was taught, "He that receiveth light, and continueth in God, receiveth more light; and that light groweth brighter and brighter until the perfect day" (D&C 50:24).

In this way, the unfolding of our full identity comes moment by moment, choice by choice. As C. S. Lewis put it: "Every time you make a choice, you are turning the core, central part of you into something a little different from what it was before. All of our lives, across many choices, we are slowly turning this central thing into one kind of a person or another."[9]

Rather than only discovering who we really are (and living that out), then, this is about an intentional path of deep, ongoing cultivation of self. Moment by moment, we find ourselves literally revealed on this path through our choices.

THE PRACTICE: *Jarom and his fifteen-year-old daughter, Anja, were scanning the example list of goals the Church had provided for youth. "What do you think of this list?" he asked her. Anja was engaged, but unsure, "Uhh, I don't know . . ." she said as she pulled the list closer. "This one looks easy, how about that?" she said, pointing to the line, "Memorize a hymn." Jarom paused.*

Something didn't feel right inside, and he needed a minute to make room for what that might be. "Tired," he thought. "Just want to get this over with" came next. "I'm not very good at this parenting stuff" followed. Hmmm. He looked at his daughter and then realized there were other things, too. Hope. Wonder. This was not just about checking things off. This was about her.

"Let's stop and think about this a minute," he said, pausing. "What are you interested in focusing on right now? What's on your mind lately?" "Umm, well, I don't know. I mean, I don't know if it fits." Jarom said, "Tell me about it." "Well, it's dumb but . . ." Jarom smiled encouragingly. "You know how Corey's mom had cancer? The doctor said that since she was a runner and because she was in good health, she was able to get better faster. I like the idea of finding ways to be healthy, so maybe something with running?" Jarom nodded, "Running would be new for you. I like that you're open to trying something new. Now what?" Anja remembered, "I think we're supposed to pray about it. But, Dad, do you really think Heavenly Father cares about running?" Jarom reflected, "I am absolutely sure Heavenly Father cares about you. I don't think it matters that much where you start—the important thing is learning to be open to the Spirit's guidance as you figure out ways to grow in your relationship with Heavenly Father and in the gospel. He's going to help you figure out what the best thing is for you to focus on right now. Let's pray and see what you feel as we ask Him about it." Anja smiled.

Things to Try

When we are growing and developing new skills, we will inevitably be clumsy and end up either annoying, offending, or downright hurting others in the process of learning. Be humble in these moments, willing to receive feedback and apologize.

Don't give up. Recognize that we all must face our own shortcomings and their impact on others if we are to become better people. Hold steady, with patience and self-compassion.

Embrace learning and growing as an intrinsic, healthy, ongoing part of life—pursuing it with gentleness, grace, and patience. Even while watching any tendency toward aggressive striving, appreciate your desire for *more* learning and *greater* growth—considering it a tangible reflection of your identity as a son or daughter of God.

Notice any fear you might have around making choices. Begin to observe, from a deeper, calmer place, the seemingly endless opportunities that arise each day for moment-by-moment choices—appreciating how the detailed setup of your life makes that possible. Consider these unfolding opportunities for choice and growth as an incremental process to become your truest, best self.

Rather than approaching goals as more things to "do," experiment with these as meditative exercises on a particular area of life—little excuses to spark new renewal, growth, and enlightenment. As you focus on the larger truth behind your intention or goal, you can avoid being confined by rigid to-do lists and instead be guided by the Spirit in receiving or creating the experiences that will truly help your progression.

When a certain goal or plan is feeling consuming, pause long enough to sit with what has happened so far from a calm, curious place—recognizing this stopping as an important part of progressing *more*.

Practice *really being here*—wherever that is, however it feels—as a key part of feeling the wisdom of where you need to go next. Watch out for the tendency to *have* to get along to a better place, noticing how that can drive and badger you unawares.

When difficult emotions or uncomfortable sensations arise, watch any tendency to automatically label them as "bad." Reconsider ways they might offer helpful insights and even wise cautions for your own next steps. Likewise, when pleasant emotions or comfortable sensations arise in your experience, notice any tendency to automatically label them as "good" — thinking carefully about what exactly they mean in your life.

CHAPTER 9

BEGINNING (AGAIN):

Great News about This Very Moment

"For thus saith the Lord God, the Holy One of Israel; In returning and rest shall ye be saved; in quietness and in confidence shall be your strength."

—ISAIAH 30:15

THE PROBLEM: *"I can't believe I did that again! What a schmuck—a total idiot," muttered Craig as he closed his laptop. After three weeks in which he had finally felt some freedom, the familiar emptiness and desperation that came with betraying his covenants sat heavy on him once again. "So much for 'being good,'" he thought. As long as he was feeling this awful, he might as well do something that would take away the pain . . . so it didn't hurt so much.*

After so many years of this struggle, Craig hardly remembered life without it. But just recently, because of the intensity of his wife's heartache over this, he had made some changes that were helping him experience a deeper level of sobriety. He had felt more peace and joy these last few weeks than he could remember. But now, it was all gone. "So much for that. I know they say you can always repent—but this is different. Maybe I need to just stop beating myself up when I struggle. Isn't this something most guys deal with?" One thing was for sure. With how hurt Jenny had been by past discussions about this, there was no way she could know about any of it. She had been so happy thinking that he was starting to do better.

Overview

Spirituality is not just the happy moments when we feel good and are on track. Some of the deepest, richest, most "spiritual/righteous moments" are moments of darkness, abandonment, and injury. A desire for relief in those moments is universal to all human beings.

We have abundant opportunity to push away, avoid, and numb out in these moments—or find some kind of distraction to take us away from the pain. This kind of refusal of the present moment can often compound our pain and cover up its true source.

Living a life consumed by distraction creates a shallowness, a meaninglessness. The ultimate consequence of this neglect, this deep betrayal of reality, is spiritual death.

Rather than merely the idea of sin that makes people feel bad, it is the reality of sin and its actual effects in our lives that creates pain. When we ignore or downplay the reality of sin, we never address the source of the painful symptoms it creates.

In efforts to diminish this pain, well-intentioned people may encourage those hurting to ignore or deny the source of their suffering with messages of "it's not your fault," or "don't feel too bad." But feelings of regret, sorrow, anxiety, or even deep pain associated with our actions may be timely, even crucial, "warning signs" that move us in a better direction.

The watchfulness Christ invites us to exercise need not be a fearful watching. As we watch our internal experience with calm, God can help us discern what is happening and show us how to navigate complex emotions inside.

When urges or cravings arise, we don't have to respond with fear or shame. We can learn to acknowledge the sensations they induce with enough patience till their grip loosens. Such acknowledging isn't the same as indulging, and it's also not the same as numbing or distracting.

No matter what has come before, no matter how awful or confused or lost we might feel now, this can be a new moment, a new day. *This* is the best news of all—especially to those who are lost. That message to us—and to our loved ones also needing a fresh, healing beginning—is possible because of Jesus.

Just like we bring the attention back to the breath over and over in meditation, Christ's mercy allows us to return to Him, over and over again, when we lapse into old patterns.

In Latter-day Saint culture, we often speak approvingly of individuals who are "unwavering" or "unflagging"—celebrating those who don't appear to show any weariness in doing good, who don't shrink, and who don't ever seem to fall.

And no wonder—wouldn't it be great to be so steady, so constant, so trustworthy?

But what about times when we're *just not* this way? And what if we find ourselves wavering, stumbling, and falling *a lot*? What does that even say about us?

Maybe only that we're human . . . and aspiring to follow some perfect Heavenly Parents as best as we can. Understanding this can bring some relief, even if it doesn't take away all the pain involved in the process.

How Can I Hurt Less?

The desire to find relief and reprieve from pain is as common as breath itself. On a visceral level, the sheer reality of suffering—and our desire for something to relieve the pain—continues to be a common bond we all share, acknowledged throughout Christian scripture and held as the "first noble truth" of Buddhist teaching.[1]

While followers of Christ have additional associations with the word *salvation* beyond the here and now, it seems clear that an aspiration for *some kind of salvation* from present suffering is universal—something human beings are *all* seeking on some level.

Thus, even compared to the golden questions of missionary work (*where do I come from, why am I here, where am I going*), the platinum question may simply be, *how can I hurt less*?

Save Us from the Pain

Clearly, there is an enormous variety of *specific* answers to that question involving a wide assortment of things that people pursue or promote. Many healing interventions and medicinal substances attempt to produce some kind of a transcendent shift in people's experiences—transporting them to another place mentally, emotionally, or physically.

Drugs, alcohol, permissive sex, television, gambling, and compulsive shopping or eating also promise some way to *step away* from what is hard—"leaving behind" the pain (at least temporarily and superficially) as people are preoccupied in some form of stimulation.

In that moment—no matter what lies ahead, no matter the side effects or long-term consequences—in that moment we are "saved" from whatever discomfort may be bothering us. In this way, we cling to the pleasant sensation (or relief from pain) as our primary source of comfort and joy.

Given the enormous suffering that comes into most people's lives, can we blame anyone for seeking some kind of an escape? Why would that not be a good thing?

Fighting the Present Moment

Escaping and avoiding pain is sometimes necessary and crucial. But if pushing away or numbing out pain becomes a constant and chronic

response to discomfort, we may be setting ourselves up for longer-term heartache.

On one level, many of the things that make pain go away in the short term end up causing long-term damage. But, on another level, the pattern of pushing away pain *never teaches* us how to work through it, learn from it, and get at the roots of why we're hurting in the first place.

That all explains why something that sounds as crazy as *turning toward* our pain—and being more present to it—can actually (surprisingly) lead to a decrease in pain over time.

Now, hold on, you're thinking, *now you're asking me to be present to things that hurt? It's one thing to embrace the present moment when it's nice. But now you're suggesting we do that when things really hurt?*

Sounds kind of crazy, doesn't it?

But the research on mindfulness-based interventions for both physical and emotional health problems shows a consistent decrease in pain *as people turn to that pain in new ways.*

It was the Buddha who observed like an ancient scientist how our impulses in these painful moments were making things worse. Specifically, he highlighted "aversion" and "craving" as two sources of compounded suffering: the first involving a *pushing away* of this moment, the second, a grasping after *something better* than what is here. In both cases, the details of this present moment are *not okay*—anywhere but *here*!

Interestingly enough, virtually every act or behavior that Christians consider "sinful" also involves either craving or aversion in some way. Whatever good there is in our current resources, circumstances, family relationships, leisure, food . . . it is *not enough*—and *we want more*!

The natural man to whom King Benjamin refers, Adam Miller points out, is a "man in revolt, an enemy who *refuses the present,* a fugitive who fails to receive what is given or give what is required."

In resisting the present details and demands of our current life, Miller describes how we so often "*seek refuge from the present moment* . . . [hiding] behind a fragile veil of fantasies, memories, and projected improvements." This kind of "a refusal of life . . . a refusal of the present moment" is one potential definition of "sin"—in which "we dream of something other than life"[2]—or at least *our* life.

Misdiagnosing the Human Condition

It would be hard to come up with a word in the English vocabulary that so quickly elicits intense feelings as *sin*. To secular society, this word is little more than a mythological abstraction that somehow lingers from ancient times and mostly functions today to make people feel bad.

Is it the *idea* of "sin" that makes people feel bad, however, or the *reality* of sin itself—its actual effects in human life?

This is not a question that even comes up for most, of course, since sin isn't a factor in policy discussions, a variable in scientific experiments, or a relevant issue for most public commentators or pundits.

From a public perspective, there is *no sin* to be found.

But what if sin still matters . . . a lot? And what might be missed by ignoring the perspectives, prescriptions, and prognoses of faith communities?

President Thomas S. Monson once cited Dr. Karl Menninger's thesis that "the only way our suffering, struggling, anxious society can hope to prevent its moral ills is by recognizing the reality of sin." In his text *Whatever Became of Sin?* this renowned scientist pleads with human beings to "stop and look at what we are doing to ourselves, to each other and to our universe."[3]

As a metaphor for what many Christians see happening in society today, the prophet-poet Isaiah vividly imagines human beings walking around completely ravaged by disease and yet wholly oblivious to it: "From the sole of the foot even unto the head there is no soundness in it; but wounds, and bruises, and putrifying sores: they have not been closed, neither bound up, neither mollified with ointment" (Isaiah 1:6).

Dead Inside

Whatever original pain arises from a self-inflicted wound, then, gets compounded by the lack of awareness that anything needs to be done or even *can* be done about it. For those who become conscious of sin and its betrayal of reality, but refuse to turn away, scripture describes something called "spiritual death"—representing a human life deeply cut off from God. Dr. Miller goes on to describe the resulting experience:

> When we refuse . . . and withdraw from the present moment, we're left to wander the world undead. Zombie-like, we wander from one moment to the next with no other goal than to get somewhere else, be someone else, see something else—anywhere, anyone, anything other than what is given here and now.[4]

Joseph Smith clarified the degree to which spiritual death involves a pain arising from our deep awareness of the dissonance between our own ideals and actions, rather than a suffering imposed by an outside tormentor.[5] When people find themselves experiencing pain connected to their own actions, however, it's more likely in society today that they will redirect attention away from this connection so they won't *feel bad* about themselves.

Is It *Bad* to Feel Bad?

If Ten Commandments were established by popular vote today, they would surely include: Thou Shalt Not Offend Anyone and Thou Shalt Not Feel Bad About Thyself.

Could it sometimes be a very *good* thing to feel bad about something, though? Kyle's father once told him, "Only good men know how bad they are," and related how "awareness of [his own] flaws and the flaws of human nature" prompted in him a "deep desire to become someone better."

Especially if it teaches us something or moves us in a better direction, then, feeling discomfort for a time could be an important motivator. From a mindfulness perspective, it would be wise to make space for deep regret, sorrow, pain, or anxiety—and consider the lessons they might teach and the directions they could be pointing.

None of this requires defining ourselves as not having worth. Even when living in sin, we are loved, we are of worth, and we are valued in God's sight.

Rather than deny sin as part of a campaign to make people feel better about themselves, this helps explain why Jesus's ministry centrally involved a plea for us to *acknowledge* sin—precisely so we could find a "remission" or lifting of its inevitable consequences.

Once again, this will make great sense—or no sense at all—depending on your worldview. If sin is a mythology like Zeus and Helena, then paying more attention to it seems a little silly. For those who know the reality of sin, however, they recognize that denying it will work about as well as pretending cancer is not a big deal.

Watchfulness as Wise Awareness

Over and over, Jesus warned His followers in the New and Old Worlds to "watch and pray" (see Matthew 26:41; Mark 13:33). King Benjamin similarly taught his people to "watch yourselves, and your thoughts, and your words" (Mosiah 4:30).

After being introduced to the gentleness of mindfulness practice, we now experience *watchfulness* as not a fear-inducing ("watch-out") act, but instead, a healthy, wise attentiveness to whatever is really going on.

This includes giving attention to the intense longing and appetites that can arise within any of us, sexually or otherwise. Rather than pushing away or going with a craving immediately, we can do as Adam Miller suggests in this mindful counsel:

> Watch your hunger closely. See how, like the ocean, it has a rhythm with tides that come in and out and waves that break. . . . Acknowledge the hunger's weight, autonomy, and reality. Don't run from your hunger. Don't call it names, curse it, regret it, or shame yourself with it. But don't indulge it either. Rather, care for your hunger. Pay attention. Watch it grow and fade. Become acquainted with and sensitive to it.[6]

Brigham Young similarly encouraged the Saints to "continually . . . watch the spirit that the Lord has put in you" and "see if you can discover in yourselves the operations of the spirit and the body."[7]

Salvation by Presence

Compared to relief through avoidance, then, both Buddhist liberation and Christian salvation involve some degree of *turning toward* what is hard and what is painful.

Out of that, of course, a believer then turns toward God—not necessarily to distract from or take away all the pain magically (although this is how we all pray sometimes), but ultimately and fundamentally to seek a relationship and associated guidance in how to find redemption from it over time.

Henri Nouwen wrote by way of invitation, "Solitude is the place of our salvation. . . . It is the place where Christ remodels us in his own image and frees us from the victimizing compulsions of the world." Given that, he suggests that we ought to take responsibility for our own solitude and "fashion our own desert where we can withdraw every day, shake off our compulsions, and dwell in the gentle healing presence of our Lord."[8]

Wrenching Our Very Heartstrings

Although that healing presence is often tender, sometimes the Great Physician is committed enough to our growth that He is willing to let us undergo treatments that may hurt . . . sometimes, a lot! In sharp contrast to all the soothing self-help gurus, Jesus thus taught His followers to "take up your cross," to the point of sometimes "crucifying" aspects of our lives that betray His will. This idea is illustrated memorably in C. S. Lewis's portrayal of God's deeply uncomfortable renovation process:

> Imagine yourself as a living house. God comes in to rebuild that house. At first, perhaps, you can understand what He is doing. He is getting the drains right and stopping the leaks in the roof and so on; you knew that those jobs needed doing and so you are not surprised. But presently He starts knocking the house about in a way that hurts abominably and does not seem to make any sense. What on earth is He up to? The explanation is that He is building quite a different house from the one you thought of—throwing out a new wing here, putting on an extra floor there, running up towers, making courtyards. You thought you were being made into a decent little cottage: but He is building a palace. He intends to come and live in it Himself.[9]

Referring to the suffering Jesus sometimes allows His followers to endure, Joseph Smith was quoted as saying, "You will have all kinds of trials to pass through. And it is quite as necessary for you to be tried as it was for Abraham and other men of God. . . . God will feel after you, and He will take hold of you and *wrench your very heart strings.*"[10]

That's precisely how it feels, for instance, when we are prompted to let go of something we love and *thought* was central to our identity. Miller reiterates: "Faith isn't about getting God to play a more and more central part in your vision of a successful story. Faith is about sacrificing your story on his altar":

> As the heavens are higher than the earth, God's work in your life is bigger than the story you'd like that life to tell. His life is bigger than your plans, goals, or fears. To save your life, you'll have to lay down your stories and, minute by minute, day by day, give your life back to him. . . . Let his life manifest itself in yours rather than trying to impose your story on the life he gives.[11]

Let's Do This Together

So, what if you *can't* do that—or *struggle* mightily to do that?

After falling back enough, we can easily start to give up hope (or desire) to be anywhere else. In moments like that, the strong temptation is to feel hopeless, assuming that even God is *pretty done* with us.

Jesus had something to say about that: "The Son of man is come to seek and to save that which was lost. . . . They that are whole [healthy] need not a physician; but they that are sick" (Luke 19:10; 5:31).

Could those *most painful* moments be when the good news of Jesus matters the *very most*?

That has been our experience.

It's in our pain that Christ comes in and says, *"That's why I came. Let's do this together!"* Beyond forgiveness of sins alone, He offers far more: even power to those who feel powerless to change. Where else would the motivation come to change when our hearts don't want it? Where would we find the insight to see the change needed when our otherwise blinded minds can no longer see it?

Practically speaking, this becomes our choice, moment by moment: Do we run after some kind of stimulation to *not feel this*? Or do we take whatever we are feeling to Him—the One who has the authority, power, and empathy (see Alma 7:12) to lead us to a redemption unmatched by anything else?

The best news of all is that He actually delivers! In contrast to all the world's promises of relief, He actually comes through for us—and then stays with us after. In the communion of prayer, the remission of sacrament, and even the stillness of meditation, it is Christ whose light is "in all and through all things" and "which giveth life to all things" (D&C 88:6, 13). As King Benjamin added, it is He who "is preserving you from day to day, by lending you breath, that ye may live and move and do according to your own will, and even supporting you from one moment to another" (Mosiah 2:21).

The Best News

As powerful as reminders of other points of doctrine can be—from premortality, to the Atonement of Jesus Christ, to eternal families—for someone deeply hurting and lost to their core, they might need to hear the bigger, simpler message of Jesus. That message is that tomorrow *doesn't have* to be like today—and that even this very next moment *doesn't have* to be like the last one.

Scripture speaks of a "new heart," "newness of mind," a "new spirit," and a "new life"—welcome possibilities for those wearied by their own past. No matter what has happened previously, *the very next* moment can be new—wholly fresh. Isn't that truly the best news?

No therapy, no drug, no relationship, no movie, no accomplishment can offer the same relief. That's what that mindfulness practice called the sacrament offers: a chance to start fresh, to have sins lifted from shoulders, and to place our feet on new ground, in a new day.

If people understood what was being offered in that ordinance, they might just camp out or line up early, like for a big movie release, to make sure they can get a seat!

Starting Fresh in Our Relationships

Carrie worked with a thoughtful and intelligent Latter-day Saint woman who had experienced years of extreme childhood abuse. This client observed that we offer a lot of support to the one who has sinned so they can have a fresh start, but we don't always think as much about what will truly allow a "fresh start" for victims.

Looking at the impact of our actions, as reflected in the eyes of those we've hurt, is *really* hard. For some, it provokes an intolerable level of shame or embarrassment, which they escape by ignoring or avoiding the persons affected by their sin. But acknowledging the personal impact of our betrayals (directly with those we've injured, when appropriate) and letting go of self-justifications and defensive blame shifting allows for tremendous insight and healing for all involved.

Rise and Rise Again

While Christians recognize the potential of *some* moments to be new, what if *every* moment could have a similar kind of fresh brilliance?

We help students in our mindfulness classes learn to approach every moment as new and fresh, even as a life practice, saying, "You've never breathed this breath before . . . no other moment has been exactly like this one."

There is such relief that comes when we can approach all of life in this way—especially when we can't seem to find our dramatic repentance story in real life . . . yet.

We like to believe that agency implies a kind of context-busting power to decide our fate. But, as most of us are well aware, the scope of our agency can constrict—even dramatically—under conditions of trauma, relationship aggression, physical illness, mental illness, or addiction. In such cases, it's not so simple to leave sin behind.

Our favorite repentance stories, nonetheless, typically go something like this: someone was stuck in an awful pattern, *then* they had this wonderful encounter with the Lord, and *then* they spent the rest of their lives helping others! Let's be honest, aren't those our favorites?

But again, what about those of us who can't seem to turn the corner in one grand moment? What about those who experience a new moment, then find the *next moment* very much *not new,* rather more a continuation of past moments?

Our experience is that *this* is where the Redeemer truly shines: that moment when you're convinced *you've blown it.* You're thinking, *God's really done with me this time.*

And then, in your despair, you reach out again.

Never once have we experienced God fuming at our weakness or barking at us like a drill sergeant. Instead, just like meditators bring the attention back to the breath, over and over, we've found ourselves openly encouraged after falling short to bring our heart and mind back to Him, over and over. He helps us rise and rise again, learning and growing until we push past internal barriers and break new ground that we can stand on for good.

"I Will Make All Things New"

Contrasted with the typical contemplative teaching, Latter-day Saint theology makes it clear that our moments are not new *just because,* just as part of the natural order of the universe. The freshness of this new moment is possible because of the infinite mercy of Jesus.

As Paul wrote, "But God commendeth [shows, demonstrates] his love for us, in that, while we were still sinners, Christ died for us. . . . For when we were yet without strength [utterly helpless, powerless, weak], in due time Christ died for the ungodly" (Romans 5:8; 5:6).[12]

Notice that it's at the very moment when human beings are at their worst (rather than when they are worthy, righteous, or "making God proud") that Jesus is described as giving up His life for us.

In other words, it's *here and now*—in our messes—where we can find Him, with every moment potentially becoming one of reconciliation, reunion, and beginning: each in-breath, a new beginning . . . each out-breath, a complete letting go.

In *this* moment, you could find your redemption. Could any message be more hopeful? Amulek drives this point home in perhaps the most hopeful verse in all of scripture:

> Yea, I would that ye would come forth and harden not your hearts any longer; for behold, now is the time and the day of your salvation; and therefore, if ye will repent and harden not your hearts, immediately shall the great plan of redemption be brought about unto you. For behold, this life is the time for men to prepare to meet God. (Alma 34:31–32)

Rather than "this month, or this year, or this week, is the time of your salvation," he clearly said *now*.

THE PRACTICE: *"I can't believe I did that again . . . ohhhh," muttered Craig as he closed his laptop. After three weeks in which he had finally felt some more freedom, the familiar emptiness and inner desperation that came with betraying his covenants sat heavy on him once again. "Oh, wow. That really hurts," he noticed. Closing his eyes, he noted the different sensations of unease and tension throughout his body—along with a pervasive numbness that seemed to cut him off from most feelings.*

"This is not what I really want. It's just not. Oh, it really isn't!" Craig slumped to his knees and took a long pause of silence to let his internal world settle a little before feeling his way to how to express himself: "I'm really not sure what to say, Father. . . . This hurts."

As he sat watching the sensations, thoughts, and emotions, a new insight began to arise: "Nothing I just experienced is better than the peace and joy I've been starting to feel in my life!" As that thought filled his mind, he articulated the same verbally to God, pouring his heart out to his Father in Heaven and thanking Him for showing him a little more of "what was really going on." After another long pause, he expressed gratitude for the vivid reassurance that God hadn't given up on him—and for God's hearing him and comforting him now.

As he sat in this awareness, the pain his wife had been carrying because of his actions—and his appreciation for her strength—also became clearer. After a longer period of quiet exploration, Craig arose with tears in his eyes. It still hurt, and he knew from experience that the residue of his actions wouldn't immediately dissipate, but the questions "What can I learn from this moment?" and "How can I create deeper and more lasting healing for us both?" felt motivating and right.

His mind raced with thoughts as he grabbed a pen and paper. Although still feeling a complex mixture of emotions, he felt renewed in a sense—confirmed by this sacred moment with God—that no matter what had just happened, exciting things were still possible. This didn't have to be their life forever. And that, for now, was enough.

Things to Try

Notice during an average week any patterns in your life of pushing away, numbing out, or avoiding experiences that are hard.

No matter what you are facing, experiment with letting yourself experience more of the full scope of a difficult situation—thoughts, feelings, physical sensations. In addition to exploring how to reduce immediate emotional distress, stay curious about deeper root contributors to the pain you may not be aware of yet.

As you work through something challenging, watch the

details of your unfolding experience gently, calmly, and—as best you can—without fear. Instead of rejecting or running away from bad feelings, make space for them in a way that allows them to pass through you.

When experiencing a flood of emotions, attempt to "move under" it to a calmer place deep inside—allowing you to observe the emotional storm without getting caught up in it. Keep watching until gradually the thoughts and emotions begin to slow and soften.

When an impulse hits that you have a hard time resisting, instead of getting tense or uptight or just feeling bad, approach the whole pattern a bit more like Sherlock Holmes: bringing fresh curiosity and careful observation to details of your physical body, emotions, and thoughts. Watch for new insights coming up.

In addition to watching your experience, notice the story you carry around and apply to what you're facing. Pay attention to how much you cling to your own interpretations—and how willing you *really* are to let go of them, if God has an even better story for you.

In the middle of especially difficult moments, stop and bring attention to your breath. Experiment with treating each moment as brand-new, unlike any moment that came before. If and when you fall back into old patterns, breathe deeply in a brand-new moment—recognizing, in its sensations of freshness, direct evidence of Christ's gift to the world.

CHAPTER 10

CLEAVING:

Mindfully Married

"Throw away all thoughts of imaginary things."

—KABIR

THE PROBLEM: *Claire was rushing around turning off lights, fumbling to put on her earrings, when she remembered she hadn't wrapped the birthday gift yet. "Where is Mark?" she grumbled agitatedly. "Oh, of course, he's waiting in the car. Why does he always do that! He leaves me to do everything right as we're trying to get out the door."*

Mark glanced at his watch. Seat belted and with the car motor running, he muttered, "We're going to be late; where is she!" He grabbed his phone to distract himself from his anxiety now ratcheting up. A few moments later, flushed and hurried, Claire jumped in the car with a mutually snarly look passing between them. He smirked sarcastically, "Well, right on time as usual." She retorted, "Uh-huh—and thanks for the help, by the way." In stony silence they pulled out of the driveway.

Overview

Even healthy marriages have strains. When we overlay these normal difficulties with an overarching belief that "this is not okay," however, it makes it more difficult to move through them. Allowing each other to have difficult moments and *be human* can reduce some of this suffering.

We all bring larger stories into our marriages about how a spouse *should behave* and what marriage is *supposed to look like,* based on our upbringing and the broader culture around us. Since these stories can become an added burden, it's valuable to learn to be more present and accepting of current realities that may contradict whatever assumptions we carry.

Marriage for Latter-day Saints is more than a contractual agreement based on emotional attachment and sexual needs. In addition to being a covenant, it's an order of the priesthood into which men and women enter to establish Zion on earth and to further the work of salvation in both time and eternity.

Especially during challenging times, these covenants can become anchor points around which a couple can continue to learn and progress while also cultivating deeper levels of love and tenderness over time.

Practicing a deeper level of presence with a spouse can deepen connection, attunement, and love.

Pausing in difficult moments to ensure there is enough "breathing space" in our closest relationships can help interrupt ingrained, repeated arguments and allow for more empathy and creativity. In this increased space, forgiveness and fresh insight also become more possible.

Craving the Cleaving

From making lists of desirable qualities in an "ideal spouse" to practicing signing a potential new last name, Latter-day Saint youth and single adults still find marriage to be the stuff of dreams. While broader society increasingly discounts marriage as an urgency or necessity, it remains highly prized in our community.

Laying aside whatever details we imagine, the broader brushstrokes of these storied dreams can sometimes weigh tangibly on us—how love is *supposed* to unfold, what attraction and romance are *supposed* to be like, and how the whole thing *ought* to feel.

Especially when we're unaware of these expectations, they can play with our minds and hearts—upending new couples who would otherwise make a great match, and corroding existing relationships in subtle ways over time.

In addition to influencing dating relationships, these larger stories can follow us right into marriage—expectations, if not of hollyhocks and roses, then almost certainly of a measurable (and immediate) increase in happiness catalyzed by life with our beloved.

And happily, in many cases, that's just what people find. It's now a well-established empirical finding that marriage, generally speaking, increases happiness.

There are some, however, who find marriage multiplying sorrow in surprising ways.

I Dreamed a Dream

As one Latter-day Saint husband described it: "Within one month, something had changed—a visceral shift that left us unsettled and more than a little rattled. With the wedding still visible in our rearview mirror, a new and terrific ache descended on us—a confusing, underlying tension that we couldn't seem to shake."

Seeing heartbreak emerge from our highest dreams would be a shock to anyone: *How is this happening? And how is this fair?*

Not only are significant difficulties confusing (and scary) for many new couples, they can be hard to accept at all. Is struggling like this even okay? Marriage isn't supposed to be like this, right?

In cases in which abuse emerges, the answer is clear: marriage is neither *supposed* to be like that nor sacred when it is. But in less serious cases, the *not-okay* mantra can rest heavily upon otherwise workable challenges in a way that calcifies them and makes them harder to move beyond. Something unfortunate happens when we lay on top of any struggle the convincing story that says "*not okay*!"

A Climate of Condemnation

Whatever pain or challenge is going on, when a spirit of condemnation enters a relationship, it can have a paralyzing effect. Instead of seeing challenges as workable together, all of a sudden those spouses are facing a crisis exacerbated by the harsh, suffocating demands they inadvertently make on each other. In our experience, there's no relationship challenge so hard that demands and resentment cannot make it worse!

As this same husband went on to describe: "In addition to the original distress (of sorrow or anger or fear) we were experiencing, so much of our grappling involved immature ways to make those painful emotions go away. That created a second layer of complication, wherein we weren't even communicating honestly (with ourselves or each other) about what we were *actually* feeling."

He continued: "It took us literally years to realize the degree to which this fighting, controlling, and forcing lay at the heart of our struggles together. But in the meanwhile, the resistance to each other was constant, with unending tears, cold silence, hot arguments, accusations (some voiced, others hidden), and grinding resentments . . . with little to no resolution on the horizon."

Letting Each Other Be Human Beings

For couples in the middle of this kind of painful impasse, extending a little bit of genuine space and tenderness can mean a whole lot—letting the relationship "breathe" a little. Indeed, just like happens in other areas of life (parenting, prayer, ministry), infusing some new, compassionate awareness of whatever is going on can interrupt ingrained, repeated patterns and allow for more empathy and creativity in hard moments—introducing interesting new possibilities.

Whenever a new couple gets married, there's a feeding frenzy of advice given. Want to hear the mindfully married advice we sometimes leave?

Make sure your sweetheart has *space to be a human being.* Given evidence that American couples have arrived at astronomically high expectations of each other, that's not as obvious as it sounds. As philosopher Simon May at King's College in London writes:

> We expect love to be a . . . journey for the soul, a final source of meaning and freedom . . . a key to the problem of identity, a solace in the face of rootlessness . . . a redemption from suffering, and, a promise of eternity. Or all of these at once. In short: love is being overloaded.

By requiring love to reflect "superhuman qualities," May continues, we force relationships to "labor under intolerable expectations," ultimately "demanding from the loved one far more than they can possibly be."[1] As therapist Robert Johnson similarly notes, many people now look to their spouse believing "that this mortal human being has the responsibility for making our lives whole, keeping us happy, making our lives meaningful, intense and ecstatic."[2]

The right person is thus expected to meet virtually impossible expectations, with a husband or wife supposed to be gorgeous, a best friend, a wonderful financial contributor, romantic, and an amazing parent, and the relationship as a whole fulfilling "all my core needs."

If you're married or dating someone, ask yourself right now: Is it okay for this person to be stressed? Or do you get agitated and overly *stressed* by the stress?

Is it okay for one of you to feel some anger? Or do one or both partners *get angry* about *being* angry?

Rather than play these kinds of games, it can be relieving when we remind ourselves and our loved ones that we have space (real space) to feel stressed, fearful, sad—and even frustrated.

"We'd like you to leave out the poorer, sickness, and death parts—they're a little dark."

And as soon as we accept *struggle* as inherent in marriage, guess what? Most of us find we're struggling less.

This isn't the same as resigning ourselves to chronically painful difficulties as "just the way things are," like that cheeky refrigerator magnet suggests: "The first fifty years of marriage are the hardest." If couples are aware of serious difficulties, it's important to be able to keep working through them, to find additional learning and healing as a couple.

In addition to easing tension and creating workable space for growth, mindful space can provide some other, tangible benefits to couples today.

Fully Present

Sometimes, as with our own bodies and minds, just bringing a little more focused attention to our spouse can make all the difference in the world.

It's become almost legendary how common it is for couples to prioritize screens above each other—from the commercial showing a man sneaking sports scores on a date[3] to cartoons about couples *not even pretending* to give each other uninterrupted attention. Such pervasive inattention to even the important people around us has very quickly become *not* a joke but a reality more and more of us accept as part of life. Given that backdrop, the conscious act of making oneself available to truly listen and fully be with someone can be an incredible gift—especially for our spouses.

That's true even if it's "interrupting" other kinds of stillness. Kyle remembers one morning as he awoke and began stretching in the dark to prepare for his time of personal meditation and prayer:

> *My wife poked her head around the corner of the door frame and complained that she had some time before she needed to wake up and wanted to be snuggled. I breathed through my side stretch, then plopped on top of the covers and hugged and gently kissed her cheek. This became a stretch in my practice, not an interruption. She smiled and was content. I returned to finish my stretching and then began to sit in quiet meditation, enjoying, as I usually do, the sound of my own breath as my mind, heart, and body settled like sediment in water, clarifying and slowing.*

In this case, Kyle consciously chose to expand his mindfulness practice to include time with his wife—not as a distraction but as part of better connecting to what was most important in his world. More than simply a courtesy or an effort to be polite, this kind of intentional presence might get at the heart of love itself. During a challenging time in one of our own marriages, on a day of mental busyness trying to figure out answers, a specific prompting came to simply "*see your wife*":

> *It surprised me. But as I paused the Mr. Fix-It tendencies and began to watch her more deeply—the bravery in her countenance during this tough period, and her remarkable efforts for our*

family—everything started to feel easier. I began to see a striking nobility and beauty in my sweetheart that I had been completely missing.

Watching the Story

As noted earlier, many dating couples carry a "story" of what it *means* to be in love into a new relationship—in a way that can tangibly (but invisibly) burden it. Clearly, those stories don't suddenly go away when marriage happens—nor do the patterns that were incubated in the years or even decades before marriage.

If it's true, however, that assumptions about how our partner is *supposed to act* or how love is *supposed to be* in marriage can cause problems, the opposite is also true. By recognizing the larger narratives playing with our heads and hearts, we can push back on them, consider alternatives, and come to find unique relief.

For instance, it's common for many new couples to cling to a belief that love should feel a certain way at first and continue to feel a certain way over time. From out of this expectation, more settled feelings of affection in a relationship can be experienced with great shock and even horror. In this way, the inevitable stabilizing of feelings that comes to *all* relationships can be experienced as downright terrible—perhaps even requiring drastic measures.

By comparison, Dr. Scott Peck, author of *The Road Less Traveled,* provides a new awareness and story: "It is when a couple falls out of love [that] they may begin to really love." He explains that as long as individuals are experiencing intense pleasure, their motivation to be in a relationship is largely self-centered. Peck suggests that when, for whatever reason, the *feeling of love* settles somewhat and a couple *still* chooses to act lovingly—that illustrates not tragedy, but truly impressive love.[4] Jacob will never forget watching his own father over the years of his mother's cancer journey as he loved his sweetheart *more,* not less, when she was struggling the most.

This can be a refreshing and even redemptive realization for any couple going through hard times. When struggle heightens and you may not be getting everything you hoped for in this relationship, *that very moment* is not a crisis or a tragedy. Instead, it can become a moment when you may be able to start loving your partner *even more*—not because you're driven to, but because you choose to do so.

Of course, none of us start off being so aware of these kinds of larger expectations. This might help explain some of the common challenges many singles face after spending ten to fifteen years seeking out new, exciting relationships in their dating years. Suddenly, they've now committed in marriage to remain faithful to *one person*—even after the more intense feelings subside. But even with the exchange of sincere promises, after years of pursuing a unique intensity of excitement in many changing dating relationships, both the new husband and wife can face surprising temptations from the lingering habits of heart and mind.

In contrast to all previous relationships, marriage invites two imperfect people to continue loving through good times and bad. What a refining test!

But *why,* again, would someone actually agree to do that? That question, which increasing numbers ask in society today, is best answered by a larger vision of how God sees this aspect of our mortality.

A Uniquely Latter-day Saint Approach to Marriage

The uniqueness of the Latter-day Saint view of marriage cannot be overstated. Western culture has largely come to view marriage as contractual, organized primarily around the emotional bonds, attachment needs, and sexual identity of consenting adults. But the Lord's revelation on the eternal nature of marriage elevates our view beyond Victorian Romantic ideals toward something far more expansive and transcendent than even the highest hopes of romantics today.

The sealing covenant, as taught by Joseph Smith, while often *termed* "marriage," was akin to an ordination into an "order of priesthood"—the "fulness of the Melchizedek Priesthood," as it would come to be known—requisite to obtaining the highest heaven or degree of the celestial glory (D&C 131:1–2). It would bestow a special authority on men and women to do a priestly work to establish Zion on the earth and to further the work of salvation in both time and eternity by assisting eternal intelligences to further their progression. Brigham Young would later say:

> The whole subject of the marriage relation is not in my reach, nor in any other man's reach on this earth. It is without beginning of days or end of years; it is a hard matter to reach. We can tell some things with regard to it; it lays the foundation for worlds, for angels, and for the Gods; for intelligent beings to be crowned with glory, immortality, and eternal lives. In fact, it is the thread which runs from the beginning to the end of the holy Gospel of Salvation.[5]

Again, the doctrine of marriage that Joseph taught wasn't merely about eternalizing adult romantic attachment or even transcending the burdens of family life. Joseph's marriage was about receiving the fulness of God's life and, as articulated by historian Richard Bushman, being sealed into covenant with a broader "alliance of [divine] beings who have found the way to godhood" and who work together "to bring along lesser spirits to become divine beings—a process that never began and will never end."[6]

Wow! So, what does that mean for couples facing tough times together?

Because I Promised

It's common for these kinds of marriage commitments to be seen as somehow restrictive and constricting. Compared with the unsettled fears and traumas often associated with no-strings-attached relationships, however, sacred promises can provide a profound kind of safety and comfort.

The spouse of one of our dear friends faced some serious health challenges for many years, which placed a natural strain on their marriage. When asked where he found his strength, this man said, "Sometimes, I'm trying to be a good husband and father because I feel like it—other times, I do all those things *because I promised.*"

Even as Latter-day Saints have, in contemporary society, largely reembraced many of the ideals of Victorian Romanticism as being important to marriage, at its core, our approach to marriage still rests on a foundation of priestly spiritual anchors. By bringing more attention to some of that beautiful language and those spiritual teachings, we believe marriages can be profoundly strengthened. For example, in some inspired instruction, the Prophet wrote something Latter-day Saints haven't typically discussed in the context of marriage (but which we should!): namely, a promise that "the doctrine of the priesthood shall distil upon thy soul as the dews from heaven" as we seek to be filled with charity and keep our thoughts pure (D&C 121:45).

It's often in the still, peaceful hours of morning, uninterrupted by the busyness of day, that the dew rests. It comes without force or "compulsory means" (v. 46)—just as real growth and deepening comes in our relationships. Rather than an outcome to accomplish or *make happen,* we can approach this process as a rich, lifelong practice in itself.

Cultivating Love

In his book *The Art of Loving,* psychologist Erich Fromm speaks of love as an art to be developed and refined over time: "If one wants to become a master in any art, one's whole life must be devoted to it, or at least related to it. One's own person becomes an instrument in the practice of the art."

One research team proposed that romantic love be reframed as an "attachment process"—a gradual unfolding in "which affectional bonds are formed between adult lovers, just as affectional bonds are formed earlier in life between human infants and their parents."[7]

Like childhood attachment, romantic attachment can also be "injured" in different ways, as well as made beautifully whole and healed.[8] How to pursue that healing and cultivate that connection is a sacred practice—or an "art." "With regard to the art of loving," Fromm writes, "this means that anyone who aspires to become a master in this art must begin by practicing discipline, concentration and patience throughout every phase of his life."[9]

Watching the Heart

For many years, "communication skills" were supposed to be the saving grace for many relationship problems. But marriage researcher Blaine Fowers has pointed out that if you take a couple with deep animosity and teach them better communication skills, sometimes they are simply better able to *spew their venom* at each other![10]

Without more attention to the underlying dynamic of what's happening emotionally—in the heart—better communication skills won't likely be enough.

All the relationship workshops started by Latter-day Saint philosopher Terry Warner and his book *Bonds That Make Us Free* (and carried on by the Arbinger Institute) are lovely examples of mindful attention to the heart. In an elegant, sophisticated way, couples can learn to notice when their hearts have shifted into a hard, reactive place (a "heart at war") and learn to gently *bring them back* to a softer, more responsive place (a "heart at peace"). That kind of ongoing noticing and reanchoring parallels the same kind of meditative practice in the mind—only this time, on an emotional level.

Such a focus, of course, goes back much further to what Jesus Himself taught in His Sermon on the Mount—drawing attention over and over to where people's hearts were and where they were pointing.

Noticing our hearts, and learning to lead them the way they need to go, is huge.

Getting Stuck in Marital Conflict

At some point early in couples therapy, Carrie will tell couples the "top secret" to successful marriage counseling: "If you both refrain from pointing your finger at your spouse, and focus instead on your own work (of self-soothing when you're upset, accepting your spouse as they are on their journey, and healing your *own* woundedness), the symptoms in your marriage will dramatically improve and you will make progress as a couple." They usually nod and enthusiastically agree: *"Sure, this seems simple enough."* But inevitably, not five minutes later, one or both of them is emphatically trying to convince the therapist that focusing on their own personal growth will not work in their "unique" case. "Look, I know I'm not perfect," they concede, "but the real problem here is that my spouse . . ."

Unquestionably, we are each married to someone who is irritating, broken, and not seeing things clearly—someone who needs to work on himself or herself. Everyone is. Everyone, including *your* spouse. When your spouse's annoying daily habits and (yes, we believe you, *truly awful*) shortcomings[11] aren't resolved after loud, nagging fights or even "good communication," it starts to feel very, very personal: "This isn't just a quirky weakness in them, they're doing this *on purpose* to hurt me." Or "If they really knew me, if they *really* loved me, this wouldn't be happening." Or even more scary, "They *do* know me, and the fact that they aren't doing XYZ is evidence that *I'm not worth it.*" The anger and grief provoked, even if we "rationally" know our thoughts aren't entirely true, feels intolerable, even suffocating.

At the Gottman Institute, respected researchers on marriage have found that most problems in marriage are actually not resolved.

> When thinking about conflict in a relationship, it is
> important to ascertain whether a problem is solvable or

> perpetual. Our research has shown that 69% of relationship conflict is about perpetual problems. All couples have them—these problems are grounded in the fundamental differences that any two people face. They are either fundamental differences in your personalities that repeatedly create conflict, or fundamental differences in your lifestyle needs.[12]

At first this can seem disheartening: 69 percent of marital problems are not solvable! Now what? But actually, this can be very freeing. The fact that you haven't been able to fix this problem, or fix your spouse, isn't failure, because fixing isn't the goal. The real goal is to learn to hold the tension better. To not be so reactive. To approach one another in more open, curious ways that allow accommodations around the hurt (including compromise, forgiveness, and restitution). And to engage the experience of holding marital problems in an ongoing dialogue characterized by deep respect, compassion, and sometimes even gentle humor. Holding tension like this fosters insight and closeness (but again, not necessarily disappearance of "the problem").

Holding Perpetual Problems

The following visualization illustrates simply the mindful process of "holding marital tension." (It can also be useful with other kinds of hurts or betrayals.)

> *Imagine a small vial of poison. If you were to drink this poison, it would make you terribly ill. Now imagine a big, beautiful, freshwater lake. The water is crystal clear, and the lake is deep and expansive. If you were to pour that tablespoon of poison into the lake and let it completely dissipate, and then take a big drink from the lake, it would not make you ill. The poison still exists—it is a toxic reality—but the bigness of the freshwater lake has diluted its impact on your well-being. It can no longer harm you.*

You are the lake. Imagine expanding your capacity to hold the experiences of life with expansive perspective and depth.

Marital conflict, your spouse's weaknesses or sins, and the average hurts of the day are all real "poisons" that can have a genuine impact on your well-being. Sometimes we must eliminate these influences altogether, but we can't prevent or eliminate all of them—problems and irritations are always going to be part of relationships, part of life. We also can't just pretend "everything is okay" or "it's no big deal" when we are injured or hurting. Poison *is* harmful. But we can expand our capacity to hold the inevitable pains that enter our lives so their toxicity doesn't override our resources. The goal is to expand the lake. Expand our capacity to hold all of it.

From this more gentle, open mind-set, couples can better observe the dynamics unfolding between them, recognizing how current triggers may be related to stories and assumptions formed previously—even stories that predated (and hence had nothing to do with) the spouse!

Slowing down the reactivity also allows room for more creative responses to the present. This means the conflict will feel less all-consuming. Couples will experience conflict flare-ups more like thunderstorms: loud and disruptive sometimes, but fleeting and not really so scary. Partners can then more softly acknowledge each other's shortcomings without feeling so victimized and threatened by them. This also opens room in the heart to see the other's strengths and feel gratitude, even in the midst of conflict. Rather than judge our spouse's progress as "insufficient," we can respect his or her genuine efforts and share joy in small gains made.

This wise observing can then be brought into self-reflection, in which each individual can more deeply explore broader questions such as, "What is there for me to learn here? How can I use this experience as an opportunity for personal growth and healing? How can I become a more loving, trusting, whole being, regardless of, *or even because of,* the circumstances provoked by my partner or our relationship?"

It is a powerful moment when two spouses can look at one another, free of honeymoon delusions or power-struggle callousness, and say, with hard-earned honesty, "I know you. I know your strengths. And I know your weaknesses. And I'm in. I love you."

Relationship Redemption

BYU professor Daniel Judd argues that every marriage goes through three phases: creation, fall, and redemption.[13] If couples can be *aware* of those different phases, they might be able to better accept unique challenges as something to be expected (rather than something to freak out about).

More than just greater acceptance, though, this introduces a higher level of hope for what lies ahead. Laying aside instances of abuse as separate matters entirely, the question is: will a couple hold on long enough to see the redemption?

The couple with major struggles mentioned earlier eventually decided to experiment with a twelve-step process wherein they admitted that they were stuck, and that *on their own* they weren't likely to find a way out. Together, they then acknowledged that a "power greater than themselves could restore them to intimacy and happiness."

They later reported that "taking that next step of turning our relationship entirely over to God is what changed everything." They continued: "Rather than *our* story and expectations driving everything, we began to seek with more curiosity for God's own expectations for our relationship, without simply assuming our assumptions were right. This introduced a level of freedom, relief, and hope into our marriage—at precisely the time when we needed it the most."

THE PRACTICE: *Claire was rushing around turning off lights, fumbling to put on her earrings, when she remembered she hadn't wrapped the birthday gift yet. The first thought that popped into her mind was, "Where is Mark?" She paused and closed her eyes, taking quick note of what she was feeling: "Agitation. Late. Shortness of breath. Heated. Blaming Mark. Embarrassed . . ." That one was a little surprising. An urge to "fix this weakness" arose with shaming intensity, but softened as she acknowledged what was coming up, creating space for both the inconvenient realities her chronic lateness caused her and her loved ones as well as a more understanding motivation to work on it.*

Mark glanced at his watch, muttering, "We're going to be late; where is she?" Aware of an angry frustration rising in his chest, he reached for his phone to distract himself, but stopped and took a deep breath. "Slow down," he said softly. "This is inconvenient, but tonight is bigger than this moment. Our relationship is bigger than this moment. I am bigger than this inconvenience." He imagined dissolving the angry provocation of Claire's frustrating lateness in a giant lake, and he could almost feel his mind and body expanding to make space for all these sensations. He was still irritated, but it seemed more in perspective and less likely to ruin the evening.

When Claire climbed in the car a moment later, they looked at one another with an unspoken, tender understanding of the annoyance this delay had caused. Squeezing hands and looking forward, they pulled out of the driveway and headed to the party.

Things to Try

If you haven't found a marriage partner yet, or if your relationship isn't quite where you'd like it to be, pay attention to the inner tendency toward drivenness and craving—noticing how that plays out in your actions and emotional experience.

Make it an ongoing practice to let your spouse be a human being, extending space and grace for your partner to learn, grow, and even make mistakes. By the same token, make sure your relationship has "space to breathe."

Consider date night as a crucial "retreat" from the demands of your usual schedules, making it a more committed *practice* to protect regular, dedicated time as a couple away from it all. Even when a "night out" is not an option, block out (think "rebounding") one evening a week just to focus on each other and your relationship.

When you are with your spouse, pay attention to *how present* you actually are and what is going on inside when you look like you are paying attention. Where is your mind? Where is your heart? How does it feel in the body and mind when you give *full presence* to your spouse?

Reflect on the needs or expectations you are expecting your spouse to fulfill that may often be the source of conflict in your relationship. With the magnanimity and allowance you might give to a stranger, consider how fair these expectations are of this human being. What are other ways in which these needs might be fulfilled? How might you yourself be able to meet them? How might others be better equipped to meet them than your spouse?

At the end of the day, experiment with blocking off a little quiet time before bed exclusively for you and your spouse just to be together: Time to sit. To ask questions. To meditate. To pray together.

In lieu of asking, "How was your day?" or "How are you doing?" experiment with asking each other, "What's going on for you right now? What's in your heart and mind?" Then, for at least a few minutes each day, let each other answer that question—with as complete and full attention as you can give to listen. This kind of regular, mindful listening can be a powerful practice in itself.

Notice when you've fallen into a "reactive" pattern of communicating—recognizing the tension in the body or a pattern of rigidness or defensiveness in your responses to one another.

If you are in a longstanding painful pattern with your spouse, an important starting point can be to admit that you are really stuck. Then, ask yourselves if you can come to believe that a power greater than yourselves could restore you to commitment and intimacy. If so, prepare to make a decision to turn your wills and your life together over to the care of God.[14]

Especially during challenging times, also pay attention to what's going on in your heart. Is your heart at war or at peace? If or when you find your heart's desires wandering off and away from your spouse, get in the practice of noticing that—and then redirect your own heart back to him or her.

Notice what kind of *stories* you carry around about your own relationship: ideas, expectations, and assumptions about how marriage is *supposed* to be, how love is *supposed* to feel, and how your connection *should* be. Get a little more curious about where these stories come from and whether they are consistent with God's own expectations for your relationship.

CHAPTER 11

NURTURING:

Mindful Parenting

"No other work transcends that
of righteous, *intentional* parenting!"
—PRESIDENT RUSSELL M. NELSON

THE PROBLEM: *Rachael left for the weekend to give her sister a hand, leaving Eddie with the three girls. Getting through the laundry list of activities and daily family rituals was not something Eddie ever did alone (or ever really took the lead on). It was largely punching the clock for him—9 to 5, and then coming home to help with dinner and bedtime. But he figured he could handle getting everyone ready in the morning and moving them from point A to B to C to D to Omega . . .*

After juggling basketball practice and dinner, Eddie felt pretty good about things. The kids were pushed into their pajamas and handed their toothbrushes—list completed.

But with tensions high and schedules tight, genuine conversation and affection were nearly absent in the race to get it all done. As he sat down on the edge of the bed to sing them their good-night song, Eddie felt the sudden sting of something important he had overlooked while getting it all done: his girls.

Overview

Even with the enormity of their responsibilities, our Heavenly Parents are not "stressed out" in their parenting. We can emulate their example.

How we take on the challenges of parenting, of shepherding the precious souls in our care, may be a central test of mortality.

The interruption and noise of children can be part of our mindfulness practice, not an obstacle to it. Similarly, the repetitive chores of family life can be experienced as ongoing mindfulness touch points throughout the day.

Rather than trying to shut down chaotic family energy, we can punctuate the day with quiet times that build stillness into the rhythm and atmosphere of our homes. These times can be embraced not just as more *things to do* but as "stoppage time" in the day's otherwise constant flow of activity and noise.

As parents, we can watch tendencies toward "chronic distraction" or "continuous partial attention" with our children.

Parents are not called to be entirely on-demand to their children's whims and wants. Setting healthy limits and encouraging children to navigate downtime independently will build respect and important self-care skills—in children and adults!

Mindfully observing the tensions or irritations that arise as parents with our children provides an opportunity for deeper, broader reflection and growth. Noticing our internal reactions to discipline problems with more compassion and space also allows us to be wiser and more empathic in our responses.

Parenting is stressful—but does it have to be *this stressful*? It's exhausting, but is it inevitably as exhausting as many parents today experience it?

Parenthood as Martyrdom

There is an unspoken assumption among some parents that what is required to do a good job is giving *everything* to our children—whatever they need. When the predictable weariness comes, this can reinforce the notion that parents deserve spa treatment and escape—something, *anything* to get away from that unbearable exhaustion, right?

As one mother admits, "If I were to speak honestly when someone asks how I am doing, I would have to say I am drowning. How can I feel peace and find personal revelation and purpose when I feel angry and tired and deflated?"

Sometimes stepping away or slowing down, however, seems to make things worse. When explaining why she didn't feel like she could take breaks, one mother compared her life to a movie about a racing bus that will blow up if anyone tries to stop it: "When I slow down, the mess piles up, and it's like I'm punished for it later."

While there are many challenging things we can imagine our Heavenly Parents experiencing (deep sorrow, searing frustration), it's very difficult to imagine Them—even with all the unimaginable parenting burden they carry—as being overwhelmed or "stressed out." Although, of course, any comparison is challenging given the very large gap between us and the divine, we can't help but ask ourselves: how can parents today set up home life in a way that's not *so darned stressful and hectic*?

In what follows, we explore some examples of how different families have experimented with introducing more space, silence, and stillness into their homes, and we consider what the added attentiveness and presence have meant in day-to-day family life.

Pausing at Home

For any home with children, two things are guaranteed: lots of activity and lots of noise. Rather than trying to shut down chaotic energy, a mindful approach would encourage the building of pauses into the day—intentional interruptions of the flow of activity and noise.

This can come in various shapes and sizes, from super brief to longer periods, depending on the children's ages. The pauses can include modified nap or reading times, quiet play for young children, and the intentional pause of family dinner or prayer.

President John Taylor once asked a congregation, "Do you have prayers in your family?" When a voice in the congregation said "Yes," he continued, "And when you do, do you go through the operation like the guiding of a piece of machinery, or do you bow in meekness and with a sincere desire to seek the blessing of God upon you and your household?"[1]

Introducing a little more silence or space into prayer can make it easier for everyone—especially kids. At the front end of prayer, Jacob's young family "takes three breaths" as a way to help the boys (and Daddy too) settle a bit before starting to speak.

Similar presence can be brought into family dinner. After noticing growing annoyance and rushing at dinner, one of our families tried establishing a "dinner hour" that started with gathering to help finish creating the meal, followed by sitting down together with a focus on talking as much as eating, and ending with cleaning up together as a sweet ending to the ritual. Less of a task to complete, dinner has become something we look forward to more.

Carrie's family decided to have daily "tea time" for after-school snacks with her seven- and five-year-olds—complete with a tablecloth and real, "fancy" teacups and serving platters. The focus is on slowing down and connecting by sharing the highs and lows of the day.

We've found these kinds of times can be enjoyable (and crucial) "stoppage time" in the day's otherwise constant flow of activity and noise.

Home as a Sanctuary

Over time, these intentional interruptions can start to gradually change the larger home atmosphere, yielding more of a sense of sanctuary and "refuge" in the home. Elder Richard G. Scott has taught: "As you center your home on the Savior, it will naturally become a refuge not only to your own family but also to friends who live in more difficult circumstances. They will be drawn to the serenity they feel there."[2]

But even when family members are in the same house, of course, there's no longer any guarantee they're occupying the same mental or emotional space.

Not Quite There

Ever notice how fascinated children can be with devices—keyboards, phones, touch screens, and the like? Most parents assume that this is because, well, the device is cool—"Hey, look, even this one-year-old wants to play with it!"

Not so fast. There might be another explanation not so easy on the ears.

Jacob's two-year-old recently ran up to him repeatedly, wanting to play, fresh from a bath in his green-and-red Christmas pajamas. But as Jacob confesses, *I was focused on the screen, trying to beat a deadline as I knelt—literally kneeling(!)—before our desktop computer.*

From moments like this, we've started to realize why so many kids seem fascinated with our screens and devices. Children reach for these devices because they *see us* giving such undivided attention to them—the same attention they are craving and wanting. When they reach for what we love—what we *are* giving our attention toward—they're reaching for us!

This is not about ragging on busy parents so much as about recognizing a pattern *we all* fall into. Researchers on the East Coast of the United States observed fifty-five caregivers eating with one or more children in fast-food restaurants. Forty of the adults were absorbed with their phones to varying degrees, some almost entirely ignoring the children. When the children predictably tried to catch their parents' attention, they were frequently ignored.[3] One person recounts:

> The other day I was at the pizza place and a dad in a suit was taking his daughter to order pizza. While they waited, the girl kept chatting delightfully at her father. He completely ignored her and tapped at his phone in a worried way. Finally she said, "Daddy! Will you please put that thing away for once!" He ignored her still. Finally she gave up and hummed to herself.

This person added, "I wanted to say to him that in five years she wouldn't be begging him to talk with her. Another commenter, Raya Potter, says it's time to talk about what it looks like to see a child's face . . . when Mom is completely engrossed in Facebook—i.e., the obsessive and maddening finger scrolling—as the child exits school doors, looking for Mom to be excited to see them, but no dice. Or, when I take my kids to eat donuts even my nine-year-old observed to me, 'Mommy that's kind of sad that little boy is just eating his donut staring at the window.' Well, yeah, Dad is on his phone . . . chuckling to [himself as he scrolls]."

She adds, "Maybe some of this would stop if someone made a video of stills of these kids' faces. It's utterly heartbreaking."[4]

This is about more than just an emotional disappointment, however. Jack P. Shonkoff, a researcher at Harvard's Center on the Developing Child, writes about how relational a child's verbal development is and how much children rely on rhythmic interaction (what some have called a "conversational duet"[5]) to build the early architecture of their brains.

Although surfing social media or checking emails with an infant seems harmless enough, there are studies that show children who are spoken to frequently before the age of two develop a vocabulary twice as large as those with less interaction.

So, let's be honest, parents—don't we all struggle with this? If so, what to do?

Fully There vs. Fully Not

In the article "Give Kids Your Undivided Attention—or No Attention At All," Catherine Newman provides one especially helpful piece of counsel from her many years of parenting: "Leave the children alone when you must and then really be with them when you can . . . instead of half paying attention to them all the time (cough smartphone cough)."

She explains that this entails "eliminating that vast middle ground of half paying attention" (what technology expert Linda Stone calls "continuous partial attention"[6])—"e.g., checking your email for just long enough that they finally wander off and get involved in the construction of a Lego jewel-loading dock, and then interrupting them, guiltily ('Wow! So, are those things at the jewel-loading dock jewels?')"

Newman confesses: "When I leave the computer open on the couch in the living room, for example—email is like an alluring other person in the room, pinging out slobbering little Pavlovian messages to me. I will be driven to such distraction that one of my marbles will be blocked permanently from exiting its triangle, and my children will sigh and, almost reluctantly, beat me at Chinese checkers."

Our full attention may be the greatest gift we can give our children. And doing our best to be more fully present to a child can be a powerful practice. As Thich Nhat Hanh put it, "When our beautiful child comes up to us and smiles, we are completely there for her."[7]

Among other things, this allows us to really, *really* feel out where a child is and what he or she needs. We often recommend that parents dedicate fifteen minutes of uninterrupted, one-on-one playtime with a young child who is misbehaving. No cell phones, no checking emails, no taking calls during this time. And no commenting on behavioral problems during this play time, no berating or analyzing of any kind. Just play, with full presence, allowing the child to direct the activity, every day for two weeks.

One very skeptical mom who had tried "everything" over the last four years to eliminate a problem behavior (including sticker charts, elaborate reward systems, harsh scolding, and flat-out begging) decided to give this undivided-attention idea a shot, but without a lot of hope. Two weeks later, she was amazed that the problem had "virtually disappeared," without her ever having directly addressed it. Another mother found that the time she spent with a child who had been severely acting out allowed her to experience him in a softer, more joyful way. So much so that what initially seemed an impossible luxury—to carve out one-on-one time daily—became a scheduling necessity. He never let her forget, either, about his "special playtime."

This isn't about getting extreme and requiring a kind of constant presence and attention to children. It's about being more conscious of the patterns governing where we direct our attention. As another parent pointed out, "There is room for the 'middling' sort of attention (e.g., cooking and keeping an eye out at the same time, chatting with a friend)"—which is different from zoning out from the kids while you're on the phone.

When she catches herself half listening to her kids, "vacantly mm-hmm-ing," another mother says, "I try to snap out of it and aim my focus directly at them. If I can't, I let them know I can't really watch or listen right then. I know they appreciate it and would rather wait a minute for my full attention. They learn patience, and they also know that I truly do care about whatever they're sharing."

Kids who grow up in homes in which connection is prioritized over distraction come away with a unique ability. One father was asked about his son, who was rarely on his phone, "How did you learn to live that way?" His answer: "By never learning to live the other way."

Finding Refuge as Parents

More than 1,000 children interviewed by one researcher were asked, "If you were granted one wish to change the way that your parents' work affects your life, what would that be?" Their most common answer was that their parents would simply be less stressed out.[8]

Susan Kaiser Greenland, author of *The Mindful Child,* recounted teaching mindfulness to a group of children in an after-school program that ended around 5:00 p.m. "We would get ourselves to a calm, centered place. . . . And then, you'd look up and in would come something that looked like a tornado, as the whole energy of the room shifted. And who was that? It was somebody's parents."

Without their own moments of stillness during a day—reading, writing, meditating—parents inevitably bring their own inner turmoil into the fabric of family life.

The benefits of building more stillness and rest into a normal day could be surprising. Take it from one of the greatest athletes in the world! In an article originally titled "The genius way LeBron James is sneaking in his rest," ESPN writer Brian Windworst reveals the mystery of how this senior superstar is playing more minutes than ever while staying as dominant as ever. "James has perfected the art of resting while playing," he writes, noting that elite athletes in boxing and swimming have used this approach for years: "looking for moments in competition in which they can ease their load and allow for little scraps of rest they hope will add up."

In the case of James, "this means finding times within games when he can catch his breath even when play is going on"—with statistics showing he moves "slower than about any rotation player in the league," with nearly 75 percent of his time on the court during the regular season walking. As James summarized, "I try to save pockets of energy when I know I'm going to be needed [later]. Over the course of games . . . these little corners often add up."[9]

We've found that "little pockets of energy" can add up for us, too—with even a little stillness creating a space where we can get calm underneath the crazy. Stillness increases our capacity to hold chaos without getting swept up in it. After beginning to make more intentional time for stillness, one mother told us, "I deal with the chaos of my young children in a more peaceful and understanding way." And one of our spouses says that practicing yoga has helped her to feel clearer and more emotionally light in a way that sometimes lasts for days afterward.

She also started doing a small yoga practice with their kids, who—especially when they felt sad or angry—would occasionally exclaim things like, "We need to do yoga!" Even at their young ages, they could feel—and *wanted*—the energy shift that this meditative practice created.

We often celebrate the willingness of Mary, the mother of Jesus, to ponder sacred insights silently in her heart. And yet, when parents consider ways to build in more space and silence, they still often feel they are neglecting the children at home. Consider, however, the powerful message being communicated when a child sees Mom or Dad making time for silence, stillness, and reading. This can help remind both parent and child that God also wants some time with His own child—you!

Deep Learning from Our Own Experience

When Carrie was in her late twenties, before she was married or had children, she decided to read a very well researched academic book on the history of motherhood.

> *It was a hefty book, and I lugged it on a vacation with me to the beautiful island of Victoria. I distinctly remember reading as I sat on the ferry on a bright, sunny day, overlooking the gorgeous water view. I read page after page of this well-written, well-documented outline on motherhood.*
>
> *It was the first time I experienced a full-blown migraine.*

As I've come to trust more my own intuition moment by moment over the years, it's allowed me to create a space around the experience of being a mother where I don't have to have all the answers mapped out in advance. I can notice whatever is unfolding for me personally, right now, with this moment and this child, and be curious about it. I can notice my visceral reactions, the emotional sensations, and the thoughts that go through my head. I have a deeper and more empathic awareness of how my child is navigating her own experience of these factors. I can observe how I am affecting my child, and how my child is affecting me. This helps me craft an environment that works for us, minimizing discipline problems for my child and burnout problems for me before they start.

Bringing deeper awareness to parenting also helps remind us that everything comes and goes, including sickness, messes, demands, and sleepiness. Clinging to one stage of a child's life, or one stage of being a parent, creates frustration. Slowing down and appreciating this unfolding moment in all its glorious, crazy richness is much more satisfying.

Observing the journey of parenthood deeply can open up invaluable personal lessons, too—including healing the big-T and little-t traumas, unresolved from our own upbringing, that creep into our kids' childhood. Dr. Shefali Tsabary, author of several books on more conscious parenting, suggests that "behavior problems" in our children, or just times when they annoy us, reflect not their brokenness but ours. She observes that parents' unattended childhood wounds get mirrored in the child, giving the adults an opportunity for deeper, broader self-reflection and healing. Indeed, when we're paying full attention, children can provide lots of powerful lessons for us—acting like "little Zen masters," as Jon and Myla Kabat-Zinn have called them.[10]

"I wasn't nervously hovered around enough as a child."

Mindful Discipline

Zen masters are famous for pushing *all* their students' buttons—on purpose! Sound familiar?

In almost every imaginable way, children seem to press and stretch and test their parents. And when a child happens to *not follow* exactly a parent's hope, a unique kind of pain can grow as parents try to *make their child* do the right thing: prodding, pleading, reminding, bugging—while stress levels rise and frustrations mount.

After one of our toddler boys ignored something asked of him:

> *I was surprised to realize how outraged I was that he would dare counter me. In that moment, I noticed what an interesting story I was carrying around about my boys' behavior: that they should be able to—right now, at ages four and two—somehow follow my every word. Wow!*

For any parent, of course, it's tricky to find the right balance between offering enough guidance for children to understand limits and expectations while also providing enough freedom for these same kids to be able to cultivate healthy growth. Within such an atmosphere, rather than seeing a child's pushing back on a request as inherently frustrating, it's possible to reimagine this as natural testing of their own in learning to exercise their agency.

By bringing awareness to these patterns in a home, we can sense when *we've* gone too far in one direction or the other: "Oooh, maybe it's time to start implementing some new family rules," or "Maybe it's time to trust her more to make some decisions for herself."

And when especially difficult moments arise, we can watch whatever sensations and feelings are coming up. Within that extra space, we can know something about what's *really* happening (including things we may not have noticed in haste), and then respond out of wisdom and compassion. This also gives us time to consider new, creative possibilities for redirecting a situation. By comparison, when we react aggressively—though we may feel like we've stopped something in the short term—almost inevitably, we've worsened and deepened the problem long term.

Not surprisingly, two of the most popular ideas associated with improving children's behavior involve intentional space and silence. The first is taking a "time-out" as a bit of space in which a child can process what just happened. The second is encouraging silence as an alternative to aggressive language: "If you can't say something nice, don't say anything at all."

One mother described a time when she heard her kids fighting in the other room: "My immediate reaction was to get mad, tense up, and storm into the room wearing my Scary Mommy face. On my way down the hallway, I became mindful of my closed fists, clenched jaw, and furrowed brow. Once I realized and changed my physical state, I experienced an emotional shift, and I was able to walk into the room calmly."

One day, long in the future, we may wake up and realize that our responses to the innocent, infinitely precious souls in our care—with their entire development, protection, and happiness in our hands—was *so much* the central test of mortality.

Teaching Children How *Not* to Get It Like They Want

Carrie holds strong to the mantra, "It's okay for you to be bored," when her kids protest at the horrors of limits to screen time. Kids get bored. How parents react can make a big difference in the lives of their children.

As reflected in articles like "Why it's so important for your child to be bored,"[11] this uncomfortable feeling can be reimagined in families as teaching valuable lessons. We might also add, "Why it's so important for your child to learn how to be hungry, thirsty, sad, mad, patient, etc."—attributes for which, not incidentally, Christian discipleship within a happy home and congregation are ideal training grounds!

In a similar way, experts say unstructured time teaches kids to solve problems and to be comfortable with their own company—skills that will follow them into adulthood.

Church as a Mindfulness Incubator

Speaking of which, have you ever reflected on how remarkable it is that children could be convinced to *sit* for a whole two-hour block of time?

Similar to the mindfulness practice inherent for anyone in collective worship, there's a remarkable amount of sitting, stillness, and quiet practice for young kids. Anyone watching children in Primary can notice the power of this experience—not just from children sitting still, but from the head-shoulders-knees-and-toes type of "Primary yoga"!

After watching parents spend lots of money sending children to mindfulness-based classes *in hopes* their child will take something away, we think our low-cost Primary mindfulness practice is quite a steal!

Kyle taught a young boy in Sunday School who was a bundle of nervous energy—a very happy, gracious, and loving child who, for the love of him, could not keep still. Kyle recalls:

> *On a usual Sunday, even while trying to control the rest of the classroom, I've had to allow the boy to bounce around—now playing with the blinds, now rattling a stack of chairs. After a few months, I got a sense of his limits and abilities enough to ask him, every few minutes, to come and sit down with the class.*
>
> *This boy would usually huff, "I don't like sitting!" or repeat something he'd heard someone tell him recently: "It's not in my genetics." I smiled back that time, mindful of my own habits, good and bad, and suggested, "There are lots of things that aren't in our genetics that are good for us, Jason."*
>
> *After pulling up an empty chair and patting the bumpy, taupe plastic seat, Jason crept over like a bare-bottomed monkey being asked to sit on a block of ice—touching the seat only with the soles of his feet, fingers gingerly perched on its back, ready to spring up at a moment's notice.*
>
> *I soothed and guided him with a penetrating but soft gaze, holding up one finger to him. "Just one minute, Jason." Then I counted off sixty seconds in my head as I continued my lesson with the others.*
>
> *His whole body chattered at first, and when I gestured to him that time was up, surprisingly, he didn't leap up and climb a wall. He hardly seemed to have noticed that his body and mind had calmed. He now seemed ambivalent about getting up at all!*

"One Day We'll Appreciate It"

With similar distracting challenges during worship time at home, it's common to hear people say about scripture study with the children, "They always hated it, but it was worth it in the end."

Is that the best we can do? A danger is that doing something that consistently feels hard can eventually push us away from it, building a negative association to that activity internally.

So how can we find more joy in this complex, sometimes chaotic practice? Like many families, Kyle's family when he was growing up struggled to be consistent at prayer and scripture reading. But they were good at starting, restarting, and then restarting-restarting-restarting again and again. As Kyle told his father in a recent phone call, he remembers with fondness those sacred moments in their family's aquamarine Vermont living room (which his dad called their "celestial room").

> *It was where we most listened to each other, sat with each other, and celebrated each other as a family. In these moments, I felt the family was whole and my place was secure. In particular, it was my father's effort to continue to try to bring us back to that place, to that circle where we all knelt next to one another, that ended up mattering most. The commitment to returning again (and again) was what I am now most grateful to him for.*

Embracing Noise and Activity as a Part of Mindful Practice

It's common for people in our mindfulness classes to assume that they can be present only when things are "quiet"—thus complaining at first about ticking clocks, barking dogs, and voices in the hallway. But rather than viewing such things as an endless, ongoing distraction from stillness, what if we experienced the noise and activity of children (or dogs or spouses) as a valuable part of our precious practice?

That's exactly what mindfulness teaches: that these distractions are *not a problem* but very much *part of the practice.*

By the same token, could the more mundane, repetitive things that occupy the life of a parent also take on a similar mindful quality? For instance, mindfulness has helped us appreciate even the repetition of everyday chores such as picking up the socks and unloading the dishwasher, reframing them as meditative opportunities. Or, as Angelina Jolie (mother of six) famously said, "I find meditation in sitting on the floor with the kids coloring for an hour, or going on the trampoline."

In this way, all the moments and experiences that "drive us nuts" in our families can become part of our mindfulness practice. The chaotic energy running through a day with children can be seen not as an endless upset but as a uniquely challenging anchor for our attention.

Kyle used to experience frustrating moments in meditating early in the morning when he would get interrupted by children waking up:

> *On one morning during my quiet time, footsteps moved in and out of the hallways pulling my wife out of bed. The world was bucking and beginning to spin around me. This, however, was not a call for me to abandon my practice, but to learn the most powerful lesson of it: welcoming the world and its activity into my stillness. There were the sounds of a cell phone being plugged into the wall behind me, a toilet being flushed, a robin outside the window, a backpack being unzipped—all visitors and companions of my stillness.*
>
> *I often embrace the children with a smile as I sit patiently, welcoming them into my quiet. I notice and appreciate the quality of their sound, what the sounds tell me about what is going on and where others are headed. In this way, my quiet is not an end in itself but a space from which to appreciate the qualities of activities around me, an enhancement of my perception of the value of what beings outside of me are doing and accomplishing.*
>
> *So, I hopped up early from my practice after a potent prayer, wishing learning and happiness for my daughters at school. Then I grabbed a spray water bottle and brush to go do everyone's hair.*

THE PRACTICE: *Eddie sits with feelings of guilt as he finishes the last few words of the good-night song for his girls, "Abide with Me, 'Tis*

Eventide." He spent almost every minute of the day with them, but he hadn't taken the time to stop, observe, and connect. The day seems past and gone, and its moments of activity and potential rest too. But not all of them . . .

Eddie knows that his awareness and attention, like the promise of repentance and regeneration, are always available, ready at hand. The girls scream and jump on the bed as he walks in to remind them (again) to settle under the covers. Still feeling the inner tension from the rush of evening activities, he feels the sensations of rising breath inside—interrupted by a fourth request to "read another story."

Instead of picking the shortest one he can find, Eddie settles into the back of the bed and wraps the blanket around both girls as he dives into the fairy tale. As girl giggles fill the room in response to his humorous voices for the dragon and the princess, he briefly closes his eyes to soak in the memory—and the sweetness of their tones.

The final hug and kiss of the evening are no longer items on his daily checklist tonight. With increased awareness and tender attention, he tucks the young girls in and kisses them. The youngest asks for an extra hug.

Their embrace crowns the day with a fulness of availability to each other. As he shuts the door quietly, Eddie smiles, "Boy, I'm going to miss this one day."

"But, Daddy, I'm thirsty!"

Things to Try

Rather than as an annoyance and distraction, embrace noise and activity as a part of the mindful practice of presence and attention—both at home and at church. Remind yourself that sometimes, when interacting with children, the adult's goal should be not full control but full presence.

When children are not getting what they want (in times of sitting at church, or a meal they do not like), approach this need to "sit with discomfort" as a good practice from which they can learn and grow.

Before praying with children, cue them to "get their body calm." With younger children, you could blow a pretend bubble to prompt taking a deep breath. With older children, have them pause and wait until they "feel the quiet" before offering the prayer. At an appropriate time, allow your children to see you praying with more intentional pauses. Before and/or after this prayer, discuss with them why you paused and what they felt.

Invite family members to "take three breaths" before beginning a group prayer. Ask where their attention goes during prayer, and invite them to follow along with each word as best they can—escorting their attention back to the voice if (and when) their minds wander.

Try making family dinner more of a ritual or practice in itself, building in structure and details that make sense for your family. As part of that, consider trying the "one conversation" rule Thomas Jefferson used to practice with dinner guests: invite family members to engage in a single, rolling conversation (cultivating skills of deep listening, not interrupting, asking questions, and so on).

Put down your own screens for a chunk of time and give your children your undivided attention. When you need to turn your attention away, draw a clean line—and let your children know where that boundary is.

Watch your tendency for "continuous partial attention," including during little-kid conversation. And become more conscious of when you are (are not) or should (should not) be available. On a regular basis, schedule fifteen minutes of one-on-one playtime with your each of your kids, during which that child has your full presence. Or five minutes. Or one.

A few minutes before the kids come home from school,

sit quietly, reconnecting with yourself, getting your heart ready to receive their energy and give them your attention.

Build scheduled pauses into the day at home—intentional interruptions of the flow of activity or noise. During this "quiet time," slow your movements, soften your voice, dim the lights, and encourage more stillness through quiet music, stretches, quiet books, or cuddling. Children may not intuitively know how to make use of such "quiet time," but by your slowing the pace, quieting your voice, and modeling appropriate activities, they will come to understand the cue. With young children, you can put on quiet music and stretch with them for one or two minutes. Or dim the lights and cuddle on the couch and "daydream" or look at some "quiet books." With older children, you can set limits of what's not okay—"roughhousing, yelling, screen time"—and let them find their own way. Or put each child into his or her own quiet room or space as part of the afternoon routine—not as reactive punishment, but as a scheduled break from the predictable hecticness.

Help young children develop the skill of mindfully holding the emotions of the day by telling them "The Story of Your Day." During bedtime stories (or sometime after dinner), walk each child through a simple version of how his or her day went, using a compassionate, objective tone of voice. Include the emotional aspects of the day, putting words on the child's experiences without judgment. This is an especially calming activity for children who are under chronic stress or who are agitated at bedtime from an overstimulating day. *For example: "Here is the story of Tim's day! This morning you woke up early and had Cheerios for breakfast. But you really wanted French toast, so you were mad at Mom and threw the Cheerios on the floor. Then you calmed down in the time-out chair and cleaned them up. Then you got dressed in your favorite green shirt and we all went to the park. You were so happy to swing on the swings! But on the way to the slide you fell and that made you feel . . . how did that make you feel? (Pause to let child fill in the blank) Oh, yeah, sad, so then you were sad and crying. Then Mom gave you a hug and you felt better and off you zipped really fast down the slide . . . etc. . . . and now we're here in bed!"*

Another variation on this is to practice a short gratitude meditation. Have all the children sit quietly in a circle for two minutes to remember their day, picking out three things for which they are thankful. Each member of the family then shares his or her gratitude with the family.

Get curious about patterns in a child's misbehavior—taking into account time of day, themes in acting-out behaviors, emotions provoked, what the child seems to be thinking in that moment, what precedes the misbehavior, and so on. Observe this gently to yourself. With this deeper understanding you may find solutions for interrupting problem behaviors that go beyond reactive punishment.

Rather than punitive time in the corner, find ways to make a time-out more of a mindful moment of reflection for a child—integrating questions, quiet time together, and a positive resolution at the end that associates silence with something positive.

Slowly decouple the cultural association of silence and quiet with punishment alone ("the silent treatment," "shut up!" and so on), transforming quiet time into something desired and celebrated. Set aside a spot in your home to which children (or adults) can retreat when they need some quiet. This is not a punishment corner, but a peaceful nook or room where one can go for some quiet time. Make the space inviting and cozy.

CONCLUSION

REVIVING:

Tasting the Gospel Again for the Very First Time

I had forgotten what it was like to feel close to God.
I can't tell you how good it is to feel peace again!

Virtually everything we experience in life is new and exciting . . . at the beginning, before it becomes familiar and routine. But ultimately a new job becomes an old job. A shiny vehicle with its new-car smell quickly becomes that used car with a royal pine air freshener. And the excitement of newlyweds naturally settles and stabilizes. Should we be surprised, then, if our experiences of spiritual practice and faith community likewise evolve and change over time—and sometimes in ways that can feel unsettling?

We began this book exploring the experience of people coming to realize they aren't feeling anymore what perhaps they used to feel in their faith and worship. We raised the possibility that some of this could arise from the impact of an accelerating, hyperactive pace of life all around us and our conditioned expectations for constant stimulation. Just as the intensity of heightened, chronic stress is having measurable effects on health and family relationships, such a frenetic pace of life, we considered, could be leading our spiritual lives to feel shallow, stretched, flat, and even empty.

If that's true, it's certainly not how we usually explain spiritual doldrums.

A Confusing Place

A couple who had spent most of their lives as active Latter-day Saints asked to meet privately with their local leader about some spiritual concerns: "Is this *it,* Bishop? Is this all we can expect?"

Despite doing all they thought they were supposed to do, this couple struggled to feel the peace and contentment that many others in the ward seemed to find. But why? Compared to those experiencing a greater depth of joy in the gospel, why do some come to feel so much less nourished in their walk of faith, while still others experience deep conflict and pain?

As important as that question is, it doesn't seem to invoke a great deal of curiosity anymore. Amidst the angst of faith struggles, many precious brothers and sisters are more likely to simply conclude, "This just isn't working anymore for me." And, as in a relationship that feels draining or the job we just can't get excited about anymore, what to do next often seems obvious and even inevitable.

An Understandable Step

It's not hard to understand why people push away from things that are uncomfortable, painful, or draining. That's how we tend to respond to emotional distress or physical pain. And it's also often our strong inclination when relationships become hard: get some distance and maybe say good-bye. So perhaps we shouldn't be surprised when this happens in our faith community as well.

While there are clearly lots of influences on any spiritual journey, most explanations of why people walk away from faith highlight some kind of presumed deficiency, either within individuals or in the Church itself. We've tried to draw attention to some of the cultural dynamics above and beyond individual and institutional spheres that have very real, intrusive influence on every part of our lives. The fact is, we're all "swimming in the same soup" when it comes to our consuming, distracting, deafening, accelerating, frenetic culture.

And, just as an otherwise healthy brain and body can be ravaged by chronic stress, and a relationship full of positive potential can be corroded by heavy schedule demands, we've seen over and over examples of how tender spiritual lives become depleted and gutted by an inability to genuinely stop, deeply rest, and authentically commune with God.

Experiencing the Gospel with Fresh Eyes

As we've outlined here, there may be another way to sit with our faith, even in its most flat, uninspiring, confusing, and painful moments. Imagine if we could better discern when we may be living in a way that predictably diminishes the joy and peace of any given moment (including spiritual ones).

Rather than seeing such a discovery as a disappointment, you might see it as really *good news.* Think about this: if you realize that your physical health challenges are the predictable result of unrelenting lifestyle patterns, you can *do something about those patterns*—potentially even to the point of reversing disease. And if you recognize that estrangement in a relationship is the predictable result of the pressures and demands of an unforgiving pace of life, you can similarly *do something about that*—potentially to the point of restoring intimacy.

Could the same thing be true of a dwindling, deteriorating spiritual life? That has been our experience—and we've observed it in the lives of many others as well. Given that, we believe that reviving faith may sometimes be as easy (or hard) as recalibrating the fundamental pace of our daily lives in a way that allows us to rediscover the subtle sweetness of a quieter, unhurried existence.

One of our friends stepped away from the Church with her husband years ago, concluding that her covenants were holding them back from finding "true happiness." After spending years of not finding what they were hoping for, however, they slowly came back. "I finally found the peace I had been searching for the whole time," she told us. "It took backing away from the screaming of the world's voices and listening to the voice inside our souls. On the anniversary of our marriage, my husband and I went to the temple for the first time in seven years. I bawled the entire time."

Could it be that, in many cases, people are walking away not simply from the Church or the gospel itself, but instead from an impoverished, depleted experience of the same? If that's true, how can we better support and minister to individuals who find themselves spiritually sapped and hollowed out (or on the path to getting there soon)?

Hastening the Work by Slowing Down

As we look out at a world increasingly in commotion, we who identify as Saints feel a natural urgency to tend to the needs of others. And so, we rightfully roll up our sleeves and get to work—seeking ways to comfort hearts, lift heads, and serve others as we share the hope of the gospel.

As *part of that hope,* and *part of that joy,* we would encourage Saints as a community to also share this mindful dimension of what the scriptures call the "rest of the Lord" (Alma 13:16). As the great ancient prophet once taught, "In returning and rest shall ye be saved; in quietness and in confidence shall be your strength" (Isaiah 30:15). How we need that strength right now!

Thus we see (as the ancient man of solitude Moroni might say today) how great is the wisdom of *slowing down* a bit—not just to smell the roses but to *ponder* important questions, to *receive* His tenderness, and to *care for* those around us in ways that can happen only with increased attention, gentleness, and quietude.

Discovering Our Own Sacred Groves

To be prepared for a historic rebirth of ancient Christianity, Joseph Smith had first thoughtfully observed the limitations of his spiritual understanding. He had earnestly engaged the scriptures by quietly pondering and internalizing prophetic words. He had heard and heeded the soft whisperings of the Spirit prompting him to ask more. He had carved out time for solitary retreat by preparing his physical space and heart for communion in prayer. He then endured the surprisingly ferocious resistance and fear that unexpectedly emerged. And he subsequently relished the brilliance of a tender encounter with his Father and Brother.

Getting to this moment of sitting at the Savior's feet, ready to learn, was a journey in the power of stillness.

And even that was just the beginning.

The same journey continues for all of us in a world increasingly agitated by an accelerating "war of words and tumult of opinions" and an expanding "scene of great confusion and bad feeling" (Joseph Smith—History 1:10, 6). Within such a world, it has become no simple matter to figure out how to make enough space for our own opportunities to sit quietly at the Savior's feet.

Like a fourteen-year-old child gazing into the heavens, our vision of what the Lord has in mind for us no doubt remains incredibly limited as well. But as President Russell M. Nelson has increasingly reminded us—and pleaded with us to see—the Lord is eager to teach us, to stretch us, to love us, and to meet us as we "stretch beyond [our] current spiritual ability"[1] and "beyond anything [we] have ever done before"[2] to receive His revelation and power.

Nephi anciently saw "the power of the Lamb of God . . . descend[ing] upon the saints" in our day and "upon the covenant people of the Lord, who were scattered upon all the face of the earth." Are we ready to receive that "power of God in great glory" anticipated by both ancient and modern prophets? (1 Nephi 14:14).

Doing so might involve something harder than just *doing more.* After we have "cheerfully [done] all things that lie in our power," the Lord might be inviting us to a task even more difficult than increasing our efforts: namely, to "stand still" (D&C 123:17). "Be still," He says, "and know that I am God" (Psalm 46:10).

Far beyond mere passivity or resignation, stillness can help give birth to new depths of power and comfort. In the space of a refreshing Sabbath, the quiet of communing prayer, and the stillness of temple retreat, something beautiful can happen.

This is our greatest desire and hope for our brothers and sisters around the world. Let us happily do all we can to align ourselves with God's will. But then, let us pause . . . and wait . . . and watch, in a place of quiet stillness, for the mighty arm of our gentle Lord to "do wonders among [us]" (Joshua 3:5).

NOTES

INTRODUCTION. NOT FEELING IT ANYMORE: LITTLE TIME, LITTLE SPACE, LITTLE SPIRITUALITY

1. Carolyn Johnson, "People Prefer Electric Shocks to Time Alone with Thoughts," *Boston Globe,* July 3, 2014.
2. Numbers are even higher for salaried workers, with fully half working more than fifty hours per week, and a full quarter reporting working more than sixty hours per week.
3. Carl Honoré, *In Praise of Slowness: Challenging the Cult of Speed* (New York: HarperOne, 2005), 4.
4. Tim Chester, *The Busy Christian's Guide to Busyness* (Downers Grove, IL: InterVarsity Press, 2006), 115.
5. Richard A. Swenson, *Margin: Restoring Emotional, Physical, Financial, and Time Reserves to Overloaded Lives* (Colorado Springs: NavPress, 2004), 96.
6. Sleep in America poll (National Sleep Foundation, 2006).
7. Robert D. Putnam, *Bowling Alone: The Collapse and Revival of American Community* (New York: Simon & Schuster, 2001), 222–23.
8. Patrick Kearon, "Messages of Love" (Brigham Young University devotional, February 14, 2012), 3.
9. Stephen S. Ilardi, *The Depression Cure* (Cambridge, MA: Da Capo Lifelong Books, 2010), viii. See also Stephen S. Ilardi, "Depression is a Disease of Civilization," TEDxEmory, May 23, 2013.
10. Tanja Hester, "The World Is Speeding Up. We're Eager to Slow Down," *Our Next Life*, September 5, 2016, https://ournextlife.com/2016/09/05/speedup-slowdown/.
11. Honoré, *In Praise of Slowness*, 13–14.

12. Swenson, *Margin;* Kevin DeYoung, *Crazy Busy: A (Mercifully) Short Book about a (Really) Big Problem* (Wheaton, IL: Crossway, 2013); and Martin Meadows, *How to Have More Time: Practical Ways to Put an End to Constant Busyness and Design a Time-Rich Lifestyle* (Meadows Publishing, 2016).
13. Jon Kabat-Zinn, *Full Catastrophe Living: Using the Wisdom of Your Body and Mind to Face Stress, Pain, and Illness* (New York: Bantam Books, 1990), xxxvii.
14. Personal correspondence, Jacob Hess with Mary Louise Bean.
15. Cynthia Bourgeault, "The Recovery of Christian Contemplation," February 12, 2017, *Center for Action and Contemplation,* https://cac.org/recovery-christian-contemplation-2017-02-12.
16. In particular, we refer here to the collective group of Protestant and Catholic leaders who have been exploring the historical roots of meditation within the Christian tradition, as well as others looking at the interface between their own Christian traditions and Eastern meditative practices. For our purposes here, the words *contemplative* and *mindful* will be used interchangeably to refer to practices and approaches reflecting ancient and modern traditions that regard awareness, silence, reflection, space, and stillness as fundamental to various levels of both health and communion with the infinite.
17. Brother Kesler added, in a correspondence with the authors, "This may be a surprising assertion, since we Latter-day Saints tend to be pragmatic and often emphasize doing rather than being. However, the restored gospel is uniquely inclusive of being and becoming, and through the gift of the Holy Ghost, sourcing inspiration and revelation by being still even for a moment. I have faith that over time we will increasingly integrate and develop meditative practices as a complement to our more active prayers which will optimize experiencing a personal stillness, an inner peace and an inspired life grounded in our relationship with our Father in Heaven and Savior."
18. Dharma refers to the canon of Buddhist teaching. See "Dharma" in *The Oxford Dictionary of World Religions.*
19. Joseph Fielding Smith, comp., *Teachings of the Prophet Joseph Smith* (Salt Lake City, UT: Deseret Book, 1976), 316.
20. *Teachings of Presidents of the Church: Brigham Young* (Salt Lake City: The Church of Jesus Christ of Latter-day Saints, 1997), 17.

CHAPTER 1. DOING: GETTING THE GOSPEL DONE

1. Dieter F. Uchtdorf, "Come, Join with Us," *Ensign,* November 2013.
2. David A. Bednar, "Becoming a Missionary," *Ensign,* November 2005.
3. Richard G. Scott, "For Peace at Home," *Ensign,* May 2013.
4. Danielle B. Wagner, "General Relief Society Presidency Counsels LDS Women to Do Less," *LDS Living,* http://www.ldsliving.com/General-Relief-Society-Presidency-Counsels-LDS-Women-to-Do-Less-You-Don-t-Have-to-Do-It-All-and-You-Can-Be-Okay-with-That/s/88392.
5. Personal correspondence in the authors' possession, Carrie Skarda with Wendy Ulrich.
6. Christopher Ash, *Zeal without Burnout* (Charlotte, NC: The Good Book Company, 2016), 51, 62.
7. Leslie Goodwin, *From Burned Out to Fired Up: A Woman's Guide to Rekindling the Passion and Meaning in Work and Life* (Deerfield Beach, FL: HCI, 2004), 14.
8. Roundtable Discussion, "Building Up a Righteous Posterity," *Worldwide Leadership Training Meeting,* February 2008.
9. Part of Jon Kabat-Zinn's definition of mindfulness, from: *Full Catastrophe Living: Using the Wisdom of Your Body and Mind to Face Stress, Pain, and Illness* (New York: Bantam Books, 1990), xxxvii.
10. Most of this quote comes from *Teachings of Gordon B. Hinckley* (Salt Lake City: Deseret Book, 1997), 334), except for President McKay's specific counsel, which comes from a later version of the account in a 1999 First Presidency Message ("Life's Obligations," *Ensign,* February 1999), in which President Hinckley added the other line.
11. *Teachings of Presidents of the Church: David O. McKay* (Salt Lake City: The Church of Jesus Christ of Latter-day Saints, 2011), 30–31.
12. Scott, "For Peace at Home."

CHAPTER 2. NON-DOING: RETREAT AND SANCTUARY IN THE RESTORED CHURCH

1. *Teachings of Presidents of the Church: Brigham Young* (Salt Lake City: The Church of Jesus Christ of Latter-day Saints, 1997), 238.
2. M. Russell Ballard, "Be Still, and Know That I Am God," Church Educational System Devotional for Young Adults, May 4, 2014.
3. Gregory A. Prince and Wm. Robert Wright, *David O. McKay and the Rise*

of Modern Mormonism (Salt Lake City: University of Utah Press, 2005), 27.

4. Adam S. Miller, *Letters to a Young Mormon,* 2nd ed. (Salt Lake City: Deseret Book, 2017), 44.
5. June 27, 2016 comment on blog post, "Sabbath as Mindfulness Retreat?" (June 26, 2016, https://mindfullymormon.org/2016/06/26/sabbath-as-mindfulness-retreat/#comments).
6. Henri J. M. Nouwen, *The Way of the Heart: Connecting with God through Prayer, Wisdom, and Silence* (New York: Ballantine Books, 2003), 16-17.
7. Personal correspondence, Jacob Hess with Parisa Parsa.
8. *Teachings of Presidents of the Church: David O. McKay* (Salt Lake City: The Church of Jesus Christ of Latter-day Saints, 2011), 35–36.
9. Dennis B. Neuenschwander, "Holy Place, Sacred Space," *Ensign,* May 2003.
10. C.S. Lewis, *Mere Christianity* (New York: HarperCollins, 2001), 198–99.
11. Richard G. Scott, "For Peace at Home," *Ensign,* May 2013.
12. Russell M. Nelson, "The Doctrinal Importance of Marriage and Children" (Worldwide Leadership training meeting, February 2012), broadcasts.churchofjesuschrist.org.
13. Russell M. Nelson, "Becoming Exemplary Latter-day Saints," *Ensign,* November 2018.
14. Gospel Library App, "Priesthood Ordinances and Blessings: Dedicating Homes."
15. Gordon B. Hinckley, "Life's Obligations," *Ensign,* February 1999.
16. Boyd K. Packer, "The Holy Temple," *Ensign,* February 1995.
17. Adrienne A. Taren, J. David Creswell, and Peter J. Gianaros, "Dispositional Mindfulness Co-Varies with Smaller Amygdala and Caudate Volumes in Community Adults," *PLoS ONE* 8, no. 5 (2013).
18. Spencer W. Kimball, "The Things of Eternity," *Ensign*, January 1977.

CHAPTER 3. COMMUNING: LIKE ONE PERSON TALKING TO ANOTHER

1. Excerpt found at 27:40–29:15 in "Face to Face" with President Henry B. Eyring and Elder Jeffrey R. Holland (worldwide youth event, March 4, 2017), facetoface.churchofjesuschrist.org.
2. *Teachings of Presidents of the Church: David O. McKay* (Salt Lake City: The Church of Jesus Christ of Latter-day Saints, 2011), 32, 36.

3. Including the King James Version, New International Version, and International Standard Version.
4. From the King James Version and International Standard Version. The New American Standard Bible also says, "Do not be hasty in word or impulsive in thought to bring up a matter in the presence of God."
5. Cynthia Bourgeault, *The Heart of Centering Prayer: Nondual Christianity in Theory and Practice* (Boulder, CO: Shambhala, 2016), 5.
6. *Teachings: David O. McKay,* 32.
7. Although not evident in the King James Version, the descriptor of "often" (NIV) or "frequently" (Berean) appears in several other translations.
8. Including the New International Version, International Standard Version, and New American Standard Bible.
9. Including the King James Version, New International Version, and Berean Study Bible.
10. Bill Gaultiere, "Jesus' Solitude and Silence," *Soul Shepherding* (blog); https://www.soulshepherding.org/jesus-solitude-and-silence/.
11. D. Todd Christofferson, "Be at Peace," *Ensign,* December 2015.
12. Adam S. Miller, *Letters to a Young Mormon,* 2nd ed. (Salt Lake City: Deseret Book, 2017), 32.
13. As cited in Eknath Easwaran, *Seeing with the Eyes of Love* (Nilgiri Press, 1996), 45.
14. Jonathan Merritt, "The Book That Revolutionized 'Christian Manhood': 15 Years After 'Wild at Heart,'" *World-Wide Religious News,* April 22, 2016, https://wwrn.org/articles/45560/.
15. Russell M. Nelson, "The Price of Priesthood Power," *Ensign,* May 2016.
16. Tish Harrison Warren, *Liturgy of the Ordinary: Sacred Practices in Everyday Life* (Downers Grove, IL: InterVarsity Press, 2016), 65.
17. Jeffrey R. Holland, "Religion: Bound by Loving Ties," BYU Devotional, August 16, 2016.
18. Edward L. Kimball, ed., *The Teachings of Spencer W. Kimball* (Salt Lake City: Bookcraft, 1982), 119.
19. Richard Rohr, *Silent Compassion: Finding God in Contemplation* (Cincinnati, OH: Franciscan Media, 2014), 55–56.
20. Joseph Fielding Smith, comp., *Teachings of the Prophet Joseph Smith* (Salt Lake City: Deseret Book, 1976), 345.
21. Emphasis added. Excerpt found at 29:40–30:35 in "Face to Face" with President Eyring and Elder Holland

22. As cited in Philip Yancey, *Finding God in Unexpected Places* (New York: Random House: 2005), 246.
23. Excerpt found at 41:00–42:00 in "Face to Face" with President Eyring and Elder Holland.
24. Thomas Keating, *Intimacy with God: An Introduction to Centering Prayer* (New York: The Crossroad Publishing Company, 2009), 17, 19, 43.
25. John Backman, *Why Can't We Talk? Christian Wisdom on Dialogue as a Habit of the Hear*t (Woodstock, VT: SkyLight Paths, 2013), 53.
26. Keating, *Intimacy with God*, 19.

CHAPTER 4. QUIETING: WORKING WITH THE RESTLESS MIND

1. Cynthia Bourgeault, *The Heart of Centering Prayer: Nondual Christianity in Theory and Practice* (Boulder, CO: Shambhala, 2016), 5–7.
2. Patrick Kearon, "Messages of Love," BYU Devotional, February 14, 2012.
3. Excerpts at 45:00–46:00 in "Face to Face" with President Henry B. Eyring and Elder Jeffrey R. Holland (worldwide youth event, March 4, 2017), facetoface.churchofjesuschrist.org.
4. Sheldon Lawrence, "Be Still: Finding Inner Peace and a Deeper Connection to Christ Through Meditation," *LDS Living*, May/June 2014, http://www.ldsliving.com/Be-Still-Finding-Inner-Peace-and-a-Deeper-Connection-to-Christ-Through-Meditation/s/75731.
5. Russell M. Nelson, "Four Gifts That Jesus Christ Offers to You," First Presidency Christmas Devotional, December 2018; broadcasts.churchofjesuschrist.org.
6. Amy Saltzman, *A Still Quiet Place: A Mindfulness Program for Teaching Children and Adolescents to Ease Stress and Difficult Emotions* (New Harbinger Publications, 2014), title page.
7. *Teachings of Presidents of the Church: David O. McKay* (Salt Lake City: The Church of Jesus Christ of Latter-day Saints, 2007), 35.
8. Brigham Young, in *Journal of Discourses*, 26 vols. (London: Latter-day Saints' Book Depot, 1854–1886), 9:288–89.
9. Personal correspondence, in authors' possession, Jacob Hess with John Backman.
10. Brigham Young, in *Journal of Discourses*, 7:164 and 11:290.
11. Richard Rohr, *Silent Compassion: Finding God in Contemplation* (Cincinnati, OH: Franciscan Media, 2014), 26.

CHAPTER 5. KNOWING: SEEING THINGS AS THEY ARE

1. Dallin H. Oaks, "Scripture Reading and Revelation," *Ensign,* January 1995.
2. *Teachings of Presidents of the Church: Joseph Smith* (Salt Lake City: The Church of Jesus Christ of Latter-day Saints, 2007), 267.
3. Terryl Givens and Fiona Givens, *The God Who Weeps: How Mormonism Makes Sense of Life* (Salt Lake City: Ensign Peak, 2012), 5. They add: "The call to faith, in this light, is not some test of a coy god, waiting to see if we 'get it right.' It is the only summons, issued under the only conditions, which can allow us fully to reveal who we are, what we most love, and what we most devoutly desire." All this is made possible, they argue, by being "confronted with a world in which there are appealing arguments for a Divinity that is a childish projection, for prophets as scheming or deluded imposters, and for scriptures as so much fabulous fiction. But there is also compelling evidence that a glorious Divinity presides over the cosmos, that His angels are strangers we have entertained unaware, and that His word and will are made manifest through a scriptural canon that is never definitively closed" (4–5).
4. Lao Tzu, *Tao Te Ching* (Fifteen), translation by Stephen Mitchell (New York: Harper Perennial, 1994), 17.
5. Adam S. Miller, *Letters to a Young Mormon,* 2nd ed. (Salt Lake City: Deseret Book, 2017), 32, 35–36.
6. D. Todd Christofferson, "Why Marriage, Why Family?" *Ensign*, May 2015.
7. Personal correspondence in authors' possession, Jacob Hess with Thomas McConkie.
8. Jonathan Haidt, *The Righteous Mind: Why Good People Are Divided by Politics and Religion* (New York: Vintage, 2012).
9. Interview with John Kesler.
10. *Teachings of Presidents of the Church: Joseph Smith* (2011), 268.
11. Russell M. Nelson, "Revelation for the Church, Revelation for Our Lives," *Ensign,* May 2018.
12. Joseph Smith, "The King Follett Sermon," April 7, 1844, Nauvoo, Illinois, in *Ensign,* May 1971.
13. *Teachings of Presidents of the Church: Joseph Smith* (2011), 419.
14. Personal correspondence in authors' possession, Jacob Hess with Thomas McConkie.

CHAPTER 6. BEING: ETERNAL LIFE RIGHT NOW

1. Dieter F. Uchtdorf, "Are You Sleeping through the Restoration?" *Ensign,* April 2014.
2. Dieter F. Uchtdorf, "Of Regrets and Resolutions," *Ensign,* November 2012.
3. Citing a 300-year-old Catholic text, "The Sacrament of the Present Moment," by Jesuit Jean-Pierre de Caussade, teaching that each day is sacred, and each moment an opportunity to hear the voice of the Almighty. (In Bob Mims, "After 70 Years, Last Rites Loom This Month for Landmark Huntsville Monastery," *Salt Lake Tribune,* August 26, 2017, https://www.sltrib.com/religion/2017/08/26/it-is-very-sad-after-70-years-last-rites-loom-this-month-for-landmark-huntsville-monastery/#gallery-carousel-9295429.)
4. Neal A. Maxwell, "Why Not Now?" *Ensign,* November 1974.
5. Richard Rohr, *Silent Compassion: Finding God in Contemplation* (Cincinnati, OH: Franciscan Media, 2014), 2, 24–25.
6. Brigham Young, in *Journal of Discourses,* 26 vols. (London: Latter-day Saints' Book Depot, 1854–1886), 4:113.
7. Danielle B. Wagner, "General Relief Society Presidency Counsels LDS Women to Do Less," *LDS Living,* http://www.ldsliving.com/General-Relief-Society-Presidency-Counsels-LDS-Women-to-Do-Less-You-Don-t-Have-to-Do-It-All-and-You-Can-Be-Okay-with-That/s/88392.
8. *The Journal of Henry David Thoreau, 1837-1861*, ed. Damion Searls (New York: Review Books Classics, 2011), journal entry for April 24, 1859.
9. As cited in Thich Nhat Hanh, *Living Buddha, Living Christ* (New York: Riverhead Books, 2007).
10. Adam S. Miller, *Letters to a Young Mormon,* 2nd ed. (Salt Lake City: Deseret Book, 2017), 95.
11. William Blake, *The Marriage of Heaven and Hell* (Boston: John W. Luce and Company, 1906), 15.
12. Miller, *Letters to a Young Mormon,* 95.
13. Mark Williams et al., *The Mindful Way through Depression: Freeing Yourself from Chronic Unhappiness* (New York: The Guilford Press: 2007), 7.

CHAPTER 7. BEING TOGETHER: SEEING AS WE ARE SEEN AND KNOWING AS WE ARE KNOWN

1. Originally from a 2006 address to the Association of Mormon Counselors and Psychotherapists not available, but confirmed by Robert Millet in subsequent correspondence with the authors.
2. See Emmanuel Levinas, *Totality and Infinity: An Essay on Exteriority* (Pittsburgh, PA: Duquesne University Press, 1969).
3. "Becoming Like God," Gospel Topics, topics.churchofjesuschrist.org.
4. Virginia H. Pearce, *A Heart Like His: Making Space for God's Love In Your Life* (Salt Lake City: Deseret Book, 2006), 47.
5. Clayton M. Christensen, *The Power of Everyday Missionaries: The What and How of Sharing the Gospel* (Salt Lake City: Deseret Book, 2012), 139.
6. David W. Augsburger, *Caring Enough to Hear and Be Heard: How to Hear and How to Be Heard in Equal Communication* (Baker Pub Group: 1982), 148.
7. Timothy Keller and Kathy Keller, *The Meaning of Marriage: Facing the Complexities of Commitment with the Wisdom of God* (New York: Penguin Books, 2011), 101.
8. Jeffrey R. Holland, "Come unto Me," Church Educational System Fireside for Young Adults, March 2, 1997; https://speeches.byu.edu/talks/jeffrey-r-holland_come-unto/.
9. Henri J. M. Nouwen, *The Way of the Heart: Connecting with God through Prayer, Wisdom, and Silence* (New York: Ballantine Books, 2003), 24–25.
10. Personal correspondence, in authors' possession, Jacob Hess with John Backman. See also Chapter 6, "Pushing Beyond Our Borders," in John Backman, *Why Can't We Talk? Christian Wisdom on Dialogue as a Habit of the Hear*t (Woodstock, VT: SkyLight Paths, 2013).

CHAPTER 8. BECOMING: ETERNAL PROGRESSION, MOMENT BY MOMENT

1. Bob Sharples, *Meditation and Relaxation in Plain English* (Somerville, MA: Wisdom Publications, 2006), 3.
2. Dallin H. Oaks, "The Challenge to Become," *Ensign,* November 2000; emphasis in original. See also David A. Bednar, "Becoming a Missionary," *Ensign,* November 2005.
3. *Teachings of Presidents of the Church: Joseph Smith* (Salt Lake City: The Church of Jesus Christ of Latter-day Saints, 2007), 268.

4. *Teachings: Joseph Smith,* 211.
5. Dieter F. Uchtdorf, "Of Regrets and Resolutions," *Ensign,* November 2012.
6. Springfield, Illinois, June 16, 1858, http://www.abrahamlincolnonline.org/lincoln/speeches/house.htm.
7. Terryl Givens and Fiona Givens, *The God Who Weeps: How Mormonism Makes Sense of Life* (Salt Lake City: Ensign Peak, 2012), 4.
8. Adam S. Miller, *Letters to a Young Mormon,* 2nd ed. (Salt Lake City: Deseret Book, 2017), 3, 79.
9. C. S. Lewis, *Mere Christianity* (New York: HarperOne, 2015), 92.

CHAPTER 9. BEGINNING (AGAIN):
GREAT NEWS ABOUT THIS VERY MOMENT

1. "The First Noble Truth," Buddhanet.net.
2. Adam S. Miller, *Rube Goldberg Machines: Essays in Mormon Theology* (Draper, UT: Greg Kofford Books, 2012), 10–12; emphasis added.
3. Thomas S. Monson, "Happiness—The Universal Quest," *Ensign,* October 1993.
4. Miller, *Rube Goldberg Machines,* 11.
5. "A man is his own tormenter and his own condemner. . . . The torment of disappointment in the mind of man is as exquisite as a lake burning with fire and brimstone." In *Teachings of Presidents of the Church: Joseph Smith* (Salt Lake City: The Church of Jesus Christ of Latter-day Saints, 2007), 224.
6. Adam S. Miller, *Letters to a Young Mormon,* 2nd ed. (Salt Lake City: Deseret Book, 2017), 73, 80–81.
7. Brigham Young, in *Journal of Discourses,* 26 vols. (London: Latter-day Saints' Book Depot, 1854–1886), 2:256.
8. Henri J. M. Nouwen, *The Way of the Heart: Connecting with God through Prayer, Wisdom, and Silence* (New York: Ballantine Books, 2003), 21–22.
9. C. S. Lewis, *Mere Christianity* (New York: HarperOne, 2015), 205.
10. *Teachings: Joseph Smith,* 231; emphasis added.
11. Miller, *Letters to a Young Mormon,* 17–18.
12. Main reference is King James Version, with parenthetical synonyms coming from these translations: "demonstrates" (New International Version), "shows" (English Standard Version), "powerless" (New International

Version), "utterly helpless" (New Living Translation), "weak" (English Standard Version).

CHAPTER 10. CLEAVING: MINDFULLY MARRIED

1. Simon May, *Love: A History* (London: Yale University Press, 2011), 4, 239, 246.
2. Robert A. Johnson, *We: Understanding the Psychology of Romantic Love* (New York: HarperOne, 1985), 61.
3. "Romantic Dinner," AT&T commercial, https://www.youtube.com/watch?v=dNQi0lI0OyE.
4. M. Scott Peck, *The Road Less Traveled* (New York: Touchstone, 1988), 88, 119; emphasis added.
5. *Discourses of Brigham Young*, comp. John A. Widtsoe (Salt Lake City: Deseret Book, 2009), 195.
6. Richard Lyman Bushman, *Mormonism: A Very Short Introduction* (New York: Oxford University Press, 2008), 71–74.
7. Cindy Hazan and Phillip Shaver, "Romantic Love Conceptualized as an Attachment Process," *Journal of Personality and Social Psychology* 52, no. 3 (March 1987): 511.
8. See Sue Johnson, *Hold Me Tight: Seven Conversations for a Lifetime of Love* (Boston, MA: Little, Brown and Company: 2008).
9. Erich Fromm, *The Art of Loving* (New York: Harper Perennial, 2006), 102, 119.
10. See Blaine J. Fowers, *Beyond the Myth of Marital Happiness* (New York: Jossey-Bass, 2000).
11. We must clarify that we are not exploring marriages characterized by abuse, repeated infidelity, or very serious addiction. Although mindfulness continues to offer advantages to individuals and couples facing such realities, we recognize these as exceptional situations in which *any* advice must be very carefully, and individually, tailored.
12. Emphasis added. Michael Fulwiler, "Managing Conflict: Solvable vs. Perpetual Problems," *The Gottman Relationship Blog*, July 2, 2012, https://www.gottman.com/blog/managing-conflict-solvable-vs-perpetual-problems/
13. Daniel K Judd, *The Simpleness of the Way: Looking to the Lord for Help and Healing* (Salt Lake City: Deseret Book, 2015), 1–13.

14. See more at Recovering Couples Anonymous, https://recovering-couples.org/.

CHAPTER 11. NURTURING: MINDFUL PARENTING

1. John Taylor, in *Journal of Discourses,* 26 vols. (London: Latter-day Saints' Book Depot, 1854–1886), 21:118.
2. Richard G. Scott, "For Peace at Home," *Ensign,* May 2013.
3. Erika Christakis, "The Dangers of Distracted Parenting," *The Atlantic,* July/August 2018; https://www.theatlantic.com/magazine/archive/2018/07/the-dangers-of-distracted-parenting/561752/.
4. Raya, April 28, 2015, and dcl, June 9, 2014, comment on Catherine Newman, "Give Kids Your Undivided Attention—or No Attention At All," *New York Times,* June 6, 2014; https://parenting.blogs.nytimes.com/2014/06/06/give-kids-your-undivided-attention-or-no-attention-at-all/.
5. Kathy Hirsh-Pasek, Rebecca M. Alper, and Roberta Michnick Golinkoff, "Living in Pasteur's Quadrant: How Conversational Duets Spark Language at Home and in the Community," *Discourse Processes,* 55, no. 4 (2018), 338–45.
6. James Fallows, "The Art of Staying Focused in a Distracting World," *The Atlantic,* June 2013, https://www.theatlantic.com/magazine/archive/2013/06/the-art-of-paying-attention/309312/.
7. Thich Nhat Hanh, *Living Buddha, Living Christ* (New York: Riverhead Books, 2007), 14.
8. Bryan Caplan, *Selfish Reasons to Have More Kids* (New York: Basic Books, 2011), 32–33.
9. Brian Windhorst, "Cavaliers are surviving in the playoffs despite the dilemma of LeBron James' rest," ESPN, May 3, 2018, http://www.espn.com/nba/story/_/id/23384071/lebron-james-plays-rests-keep-cleveland-cavaliers-hopes-alive.
10. Jon Kabat-Zinn and Myla Kabat-Zinn, *Everyday Blessings: The Inner Work of Mindful Parenting* (New York: Hachette Books, 2010), 98.
11. Lois M. Collins, "Why it's so important for your child to be bored," *Deseret News*, August 2019; https://www.deseretnews.com/article/900013330/why-its-so-important-for-your-child-to-be-bored.html.

CONCLUSION. REVIVING: TASTING THE GOSPEL AGAIN FOR THE VERY FIRST TIME

1. Russell M. Nelson, "Revelation for the Church, Revelation for Our Lives," *Ensign,* May 2018.
2. Russell M. Nelson, "Drawing the Power of Jesus Christ into Our Lives," *Ensign,* May 2017.

ABOUT THE AUTHORS

JACOB Z. HESS, PhD, is an MBSR Instructor trained through the Center for Mindfulness at the University of Massachusetts Medical School, and he has taught both adult and teen classes for years. Jacob has helped create online mindfulness-based classes for those facing depression, anxiety, and compulsive pornography use. He is on the board of the National Coalition of Dialogue & Deliberation and has studied mindful listening across socio-political disagreements for a decade. Jacob lives in Paradise, Utah, with his wife, Monique, nine chickens, three cats, and four boys who make sure their daddy's own stillness gets interrupted every five minutes or so.

CARRIE L. SKARDA, PsyD, is a psychologist in private practice in Salt Lake City, Utah. She has provided individual and couples therapy, with particular interest in attachment trauma and mindfulness, for the last eighteen years. She was the director for training at the Antioch facility of Kaiser Permanente HMO in California, and has facilitated numerous therapy groups on such topics as depression, personality disorders, work stress, crisis management, and parenting. As a facilitator at Sixteen Stones Center for Growth, LLC, she has taught workshops on mindfulness, mindful eating, and forgiveness. Carrie has been studying and practicing mindfulness and formal meditation for over ten years. She is a bit obsessed with Jerusalem, is joyfully married with two young children, and enjoys serving as Primary president in her ward and re-modeling her 1904 house.

KYLE D. ANDERSON, PhD, is the Director of the Center of Global Citizenship at Centre College, a small liberal arts college outside of Lexington, Kentucky. Kyle helped to found the college's Meditation Centre group and hosts contemplative pedagogy workshops for university instructors across the southern U.S. He regularly integrates mindfulness practices into his higher education classrooms and Church callings. Kyle is a world traveler, educator, traveler, and writer. He lives in Danville, Kentucky, with his wife, Jenny, and three daughters who love their nighttime ritual of song and gratitude meditation.

TY R. MANSFIELD, PhD, is a practicing marriage and family therapist and an adjunct instructor in Religious Education at Brigham Young University. Ty completed his undergraduate work in Asian Studies and has been actively practicing mindfulness for over ten years, and he is currently in the process of certification with Jack Kornfield and Tara Brach in their Mindfulness Meditation Teacher training program. Ty has also been actively cultivating space for more mindful listening in the area of conflicting views on sexuality and gender for the last decade through his work at North Star International and the Reconciliation and Growth Project. Ty and his wife, Danielle, and their five children live in Provo, Utah.